# World Wide What?

# World Wide What?

## Understanding the Web for Health, Wealth, Friends, and More!

*Discover how the Web will change your life!*

Niall Caldwell, Ph.D.

Georgios Petalotis, MA.

Ronald Taub, hPh.D.

Copyright ©2000 by Triumph Books. All rights reserved.

No part of this publication may be reproduced, stored in a retrieval system, or transmitted, in any form by any means, electronic, mechanical, photocopying, or otherwise, without the prior written permission of the publisher, Triumph Books, 601 South LaSalle Street, Suite 500, Chicago, Illinois 60605.

Library of Congress Cataloging-in-Publication Data

Caldwell, Niall.

World wide what? : understanding the Web for health, wealth, friends, and more! : discover how the Web will change your life! / Niall Caldwell, Georgios Petalotis, Ronald Taub.

p. cm.

ISBN 1-57243-405-8

1. World Wide Web. 2. Internet (Computer network) I. Petalotis, Georgios. II Taub, Ronald. III. Title.

TK5105.888. C344 2000

025.04—dc21                                                                                    00-032548

This book is available in quantity at special discounts for your group or organization. For further information, contact:

Triumph Books
601 South LaSalle Street
Chicago, Illinois 60605
(312) 939-3330
Fax (312) 663-3557

Trademarked names are cited only for the benefit of the trademark owner and for editorial purposes. The authors have tried to use tradenames correctly, recognizing that site addresses or their contents change, and that they may be incorrectly listed or omitted.

The statements contained are solely the opinions of the authors, and they disclaim any warranty.

Printed in Canada.

ISBN 1-57243-405-8

Book design by Amy Flammang.
Cover design by Ken Krull & Associates.
Illustrations by Jarvis Fiedler.

# Acknowledgements

**Thanks to:** All those who helped us prepare this book, including the many companies who gave us permission to reprint their Web pages and the students at the University of North London.

Special thanks to: Greg Brown; Lynn Daniels; Debbie Riley; Ethel, Zisl, Marcia Jean, and Liba Taub; Leonard, Minna, and Hannah Loventhal; and Mary Wisniewski Holden. They read, offered suggestions, and helped in the preparation of the manuscript. Thanks to Ken Krull & Associates for the cover design, and to Jarvis Fiedler for the illustrations.

We also wish to thank our publisher Mitch Rogatz and editor Heidi Hill.

## *Table of Contents*

**Introduction** ...................................................................1

**Chapter 1**  What You Should Know about the World Wide Web ..............................5

**Chapter 2**  Improving Your Health on the Web ............................................19

**Chapter 3**  Buying on the Web ...............................29

**Chapter 4**  Selling on the Web ...............................41

**Chapter 5**  Investing on the Web ...........................49

**Chapter 6**  Security on the Web .............................57

**Chapter 7**  Making Friends on the Web ................61

**Chapter 8**  Advertising on the Web .......................65

**Chapter 9**  And More ..............................................81

**Chapter 10**  The Government and the Web ..........89

**Chapter 11**  Web Technology and the Future .......97

**Author Biographies** ...............................................104

# **Introduction**

Think about all the innovations that have changed the way we live. Think about television, twenty-four-hour news, jet planes, and home freezers. Now think about the World Wide Web and how it will create more change in the next five years of your life because it will affect almost everything you do.

Before the Industrial Revolution, most people worked at home. Whether they made saddles, horseshoes, or clothing, their workshops were in their homes and their families saw them at work. Often, members of the same family worked together at the same trade.

But a big change came with the Industrial Revolution. Instead of working at home, many people, particularly men, began to go outside of the home for work. They would spend ten hours or more away from home. Their wives and children rarely saw what it was they were doing. As time went by, the family became more and more separated from the worker and his activities.

Today, that is all changing. For the first time since the eighteenth century, the trend is to work at home — this time aided by cellular phones, faxes, and, especially, computers. With the advent of the Internet and the World Wide Web, people are talking to each other and working in a way that was never before possible. The Web makes communication less costly. It offers sound, motion, printed documents, and interaction all at the same time.

The Web is not only changing the way we work, but the way we shop, learn, and make friends.

Change is not easy to deal with. In fact, it is often a shock. When the Eiffel Tower was completed in 1889, most of the population of the world had never been more than forty feet off the ground. This manmade structure built for the Paris World's Fair topped out at 1,056 feet. It was an instant success as millions wanted a view of the earth from its tower. Only eighty years later, man would view the entire earth from the moon.

## Introduction

Now the Internet and the World Wide Web offer people a way to communicate with the whole world through their computers. Through the Internet and the Web, the world has become our marketplace and our town square, where we can buy products, meet people, and gather information.

In the chapters that follow we will try to explain how the Web can enhance your health, wealth, friends, and more. We will also explain what the Web is, how it really works, where you can try it, and what it costs. We'll also try to predict how it will affect your future.

# CHAPTER 1

## What You Should Know about the World Wide Web

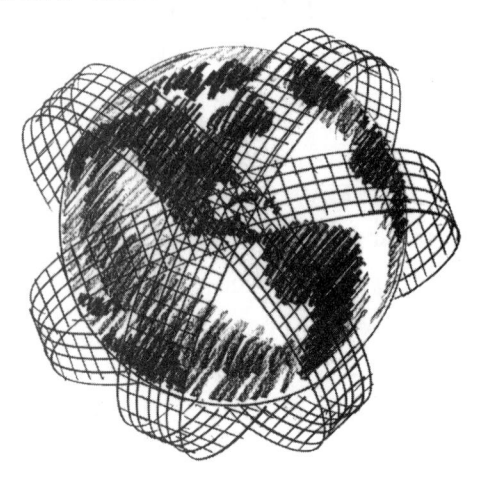

### History of the World Wide Web

An outgrowth of the Internet, the World Wide Web is a system for moving information between computers. The Internet can be compared to a power station that generates electricity and then transmits it over power lines to local areas where it is redistributed to homes — similar to the way a telephone works.

The Internet was devised by the Advanced Research Projects Agency as a research and defense network that was created for the U.S. Department of Defense in the early 1970s. It enabled scientists and researchers to communicate and exchange data and was expanded by the National Science Foundation.

The World Wide Web was developed from the Internet in 1989 by physicist Tim Berners-Lee, who was employed with the European Nuclear Research Centre (CERN) in Switzerland. CERN describes the World Wide Web as a seamless world in which information from any source can be accessed in a consistent and simple way.

The name "World Wide Web" comes from the fact that the information — sound, text, pictures, and animation — that is part of a web document may come from all over the world. For example, text from a book housed in London and a sound selection housed in Tokyo may be part of a single web document that provides links to documents in India, Costa Rica, and Michigan. In this way, a single document can seem to stretch weblike throughout the world. When users access the document in New York, all the components are instantly pulled from various locations and integrated in the document displayed to the user on the monitor, or screen. This is similar to TV programs that combine interviews with a number of people, each in a different location, all talking to one interviewer.

Essentially, the Web is an organization of files on the Internet. This means that when users are on the WWW, they are always on the Internet. But the reverse is not true. A user can be on the Internet and not the

# What You Should Know about the World Wide Web    7

WWW. Internet users who are using e-mail or newsgroups are not on the WWW unless they connect via a WWW connection, such as AOL, CompuServe, Prodigy, Yahoo, or MSN.

## How the World Wide Web Works

The World Wide Web is a collection of pages like those in a book — except that the pages can have moving pictures and sound. Just as there are many different kinds of books, so there are many different web pages. Parts of a page can be activated to allow you to see and hear other pages. This is usually accomplished by the use of a hand-controlled device (mouse) that moves a hand or arrow on the screen (monitor).

The Web works in the following manner. Messages are sent from your computer or Web tool through a series of interconnecting lines to another computer or Web tool which contains the information that you are requesting, or receives the information that you are sending. The information can be transmitted through phone lines, power lines, cables such as those used for television transmissions, and even through satellite radio waves.

Currently there is a big move to use cable lines because they are much faster than telephone lines for this purpose.

**8　Chapter 1**

The following graphic illustrates how a message is sent or received through the Web:

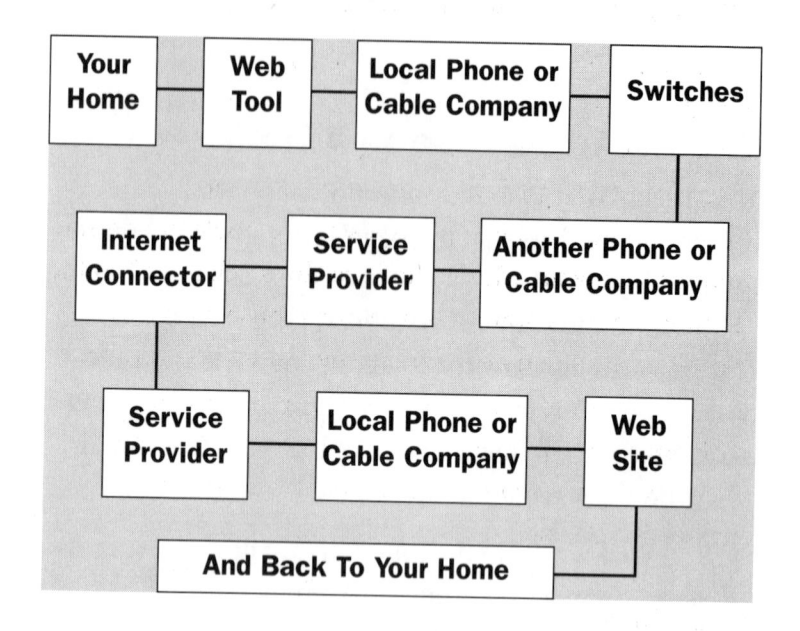

| Your Home | Web Tool | Local Phone or Cable Company | Switches |
|---|---|---|---|

| Internet Connector | Service Provider | Another Phone or Cable Company |
|---|---|---|

| Service Provider | Local Phone or Cable Company | Web Site |
|---|---|---|

| And Back To Your Home |
|---|

A Website is a collection of Web files on a particular subject that includes a beginning file called a home page. For example, each company, organization, or individual that has a Website has a single address that they give to the users. This is the home page address. From the home page a user can get to all the other pages on the site. For example, the Website for IBM has the home page address of http://www.ibm.com.

In the United States, there are three primary groups of Web addresses, each defined by a specific suffix. Most of us are familiar with "dot com" or as it is written, .com, which is an address of a company. Educational institutions such as universities and schools are defined

# What You Should Know about the World Wide Web

by the suffix .edu as in the address for Northwestern University, NWU.edu. Lastly, government and non-profit organizations use the suffix .org.

Suppose you are on a Website about sailboats. The Website home page may contain headings about different kinds of sailboats. These headings may be compared to a table of contents in a book. But instead of having to flip through the pages of the book to find the chapter you want, all you have to do is "click on" to the chapter that you want. Using your mouse, you can move the onscreen arrow to the heading you want to see — say, "American sailboats." By using the mouse to click onto that area, you can be taken from the "home page" of the sailboats Website to a "chapter" about American sailboats. This connection is called a link. Thus you can move from page to page or even to sections of a page.

A Website is rather easily confused with a Webserver. A server is a computer that holds the files for one or more sites. A very large Website may reside on a number of servers that may be in different geographic locations. IBM is a good example, since its Websites consist of thousands of files, spread out over many servers in worldwide locations.

The Web uses a protocol called /http/ to exchange information between computers. The Web transfers material on any computer into a common language so that information can be exchanged between computers connected worldwide.

Besides handling the normal capabilities of the Internet, the WWW also offers several new capabilities. The first and foremost is the ability to have hypertext documents. Hypertext is computer text that is connected to another computer. To return to the sailboats example, suppose you are reading about sailboats on the sailboat Website and you see the highlighted phrase "Australian sailboat races." To access hypertext, a user needs to place the cursor (arrow controlled by the mouse) on that word and click the mouse button. The computer or Web access device will automatically go to the connection on Australian sailboat races — into another Website altogether.

Hypertext was the main concept that led to the invention of the World Wide Web.

The WWW is accessed by programs called browsers. A browser can be graphical or text-based and can make the Internet easier to use and more intuitive. Most graphic browsers allow users to view pictures and the text of a document.

Internet Explorer and Netscape Navigator are two such popular browsers. A graphical browser allows the user to view images on his or her computer, point-and-click with a mouse to select hypertext links, and use drop-down menus (menus that appear on screen) and toolbar buttons (icons to click on) to navigate and access resources on the Internet.

# What You Should Know about the World Wide Web

The following figure illustrates the connections.

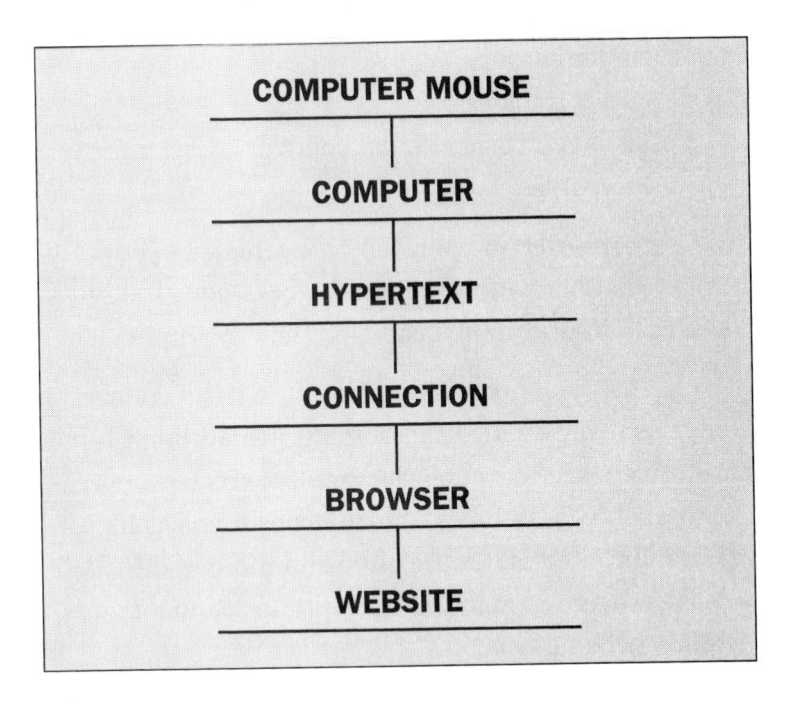

```
COMPUTER MOUSE
      |
   COMPUTER
      |
   HYPERTEXT
      |
   CONNECTION
      |
    BROWSER
      |
    WEBSITE
```

## Why are the Internet and the Web Used?

The Internet has been increasingly used as a low-cost global communication medium for knowledge sharing.

Additional applications include:

- Electronic mail and file transfer, including graphics, between companies, organizations, academia, and individuals;
- Remote access to many commercial subscription bases and public databases;
- Newsgroups, which enable electronic conferencing;

- The exchange of news and information through thousands of electronic bulletin boards or discussion groups;
- Funds transfer;
- Managed corporate data network service for companies.

Using the Web in your daily life can affect your health, wealth, relationships, and more, as we'll discuss more fully in upcoming chapters.

The Web is a global market because it can connect computers worldwide. For example, just adding China and India to the computer marketplace creates a potential market of eight times as many consumers as there are in the United States. As more and more of the world's citizens gain access to computers, a giant marketplace is being created.

Television may become the access device for much of the world. For example, China has approximately twelve million personal computers and 450 million televisions. Increased WebTV use may bring economic and educational progress to the isolated regions of the world.

Guesstimates of total business on the Web vary greatly. Including business-to-business and retail sales, the low estimates are in the billions of dollars and the high estimates are in the trillions of dollars.

As more and more countries make the Web available to their citizens, shopping will become more and more worldwide. We can expect gigantic increases in the numbers of people on the Web.

Most online shoppers currently are men, but the numbers of women shoppers are expected to increase dramatically. Women shopping on the Web spend twice as much as men. They buy jewelry, apparel, flowers, gifts, beauty and drug items, books and music, travel items, computer hardware, and software. The number of items is growing continuously as new companies are formed and more companies add Websites to their retail operations.

## Where Can You Try the Web?

If you want to try the WWW to see and feel what it's like, go to the public library. Most have computers and instructions on how to use them. Some libraries give classes in using the WWW, and many libraries have staff on hand to help you get started. Usually Web access at the library is free, although some libraries may charge for printing information if you want a paper copy.

Bill Gates, Chairman of Microsoft Corp., and his wife Melinda recently established the Gates Learning Foundation. They have donated $1.3 billion to equip libraries in all fifty states with computers and Internet access.

Web centers are opening all across the country. For example, I-Works, Inc., is establishing one thousand Web centers in the Chicago area. Digital Seas is installing Web centers on cruise ships using wireless technology. Many hotels and resorts have added computer and Web facilities.

## Chapter 1

Britain plans to connect every classroom to the Web and has launched a national network to give every child an e-mail address.

## What Does It Cost?

Web access is not limited to owners of computers. Web TV makes it possible to use your TV set as a monitor with a Web tool connection device to send and receive e-mail and connect to most other sites. With computer prices and connection prices falling, some companies now offer free computers and connection devices when you sign up for access at a monthly fee of $9.95 to $21.95. Other companies are offering free access or rebates of $400 and more if you purchase a computer or access device.

## What You Can Do on the Web

- Send messages by e-mail
- Explore hobbies and special areas of interest
- Get reports of the latest news
- Look for houses and apartments
- Find jobs
- Look for entertainment
- Shop for and sell products, services, and almost anything else you can think of from approximately one billion Web pages
- Locate information and research on almost any topic by entering related words

A word of caution: You cannot rely on everything you hear or read on the Web. You must evaluate the reliability of the source.

**Note:** In the following pages the words "Internet" and "Web" have been used interchangeably, as have the words "computer," "Web tool," and "Web-access device."

*The following three pages provide an example of a Website.*

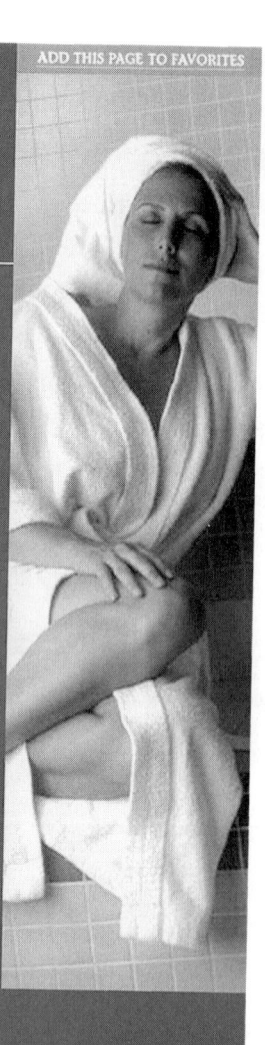

Example of Web page. Click on "What is Canyon Ranch?"

## What You Should Know about the World Wide Web 17

### CANYON RANCH HOME

# CANYON RANCH.

## WHAT IS CANYON RANCH?

Come to a place where you can soar above the day-to-day and see things in a new perspective. In tranquil settings, discover possibilities you didn't know existed. Experience the best in healthy living and learn how to make it practical - for life.

Since 1979, Canyon Ranch has set the standard for health spas as the quintessential health and fitness choice. Today, you can experience Canyon Ranch at:

- Destination resorts in two exquisite settings - the inspiring Sonoran Desert in Tucson, Arizona and the majestic Berkshire Mountains of Lenox, Massachusetts.
- An ultramodern SpaClub fitness and health facility at The Venetian Resort-Hotel-Casino in Las Vegas, Nevada.

At our health resorts, you can choose from a rich array of programs and services that have made Canyon Ranch the overwhelming best spa choice among readers of *Condé Nast Traveler* magazine throughout the 1990s. At our SpaClub you'll get a taste of what has made us a world leader in health and fitness.

With any Canyon Ranch experience you'll find all the elements of a healthy lifestyle including:

- Spa services
- Fitness activities
- Health and wellness services
- Nutrition consultations and workshops
- Nutritious gourmet cuisine

Learn to live your best while having a great time - continue through our website or call Canyon Ranch at 800-742-9000.

Listen to an audio message. Click here.

BACK TO TOP

And this page comes on the monitor. Now click on Health and wellness services.

## Chapter 1

### CANYON RANCH HOME

# CANYON RANCH.
#### HEALTH RESORTS

## SPECIAL HEALTH-FOCUSED STAYS

Canyon Ranch Health Resorts have set the standards for healthy vacations for nearly 20 years. Whether you choose our resort in lush desert foothills of Tucson, Arizona, or the pastoral rolling Berkshire Mountains of Lenox, Massachusetts, you have the opportunity to focus your stay on a health related issue - anything from weight loss to smoking cessation and stress management to grief. If you are ready to make the commitment to a healthier lifestyle, we have programs and resources to help.

- LIFE ENHANCEMENT PROGRAM
- SPECIALTY WEEKS
- SPECIAL HEALTH PACKAGES

CLIP & SEND THIS PAGE TO A FRIEND

BACK TO TOP

### LIFE ENHANCEMENT PROGRAM®

**TUCSON, ARIZONA**

In Tucson, the week-long Life Enhancement Program represents the essence of Canyon Ranch. Housed in its own facility, this in-depth program focuses on self-discovery, preventive care and lifestyle habits that keep you feeling your best all your life. Thousands of people have completed the Life Enhancement Program and gone on to make significant lifestyle changes. The Life Enhancement Program is offered throughout the year.

BACK TO TOP

### SPECIALTY WEEKS

**TUCSON, ARIZONA**

Specialty weeks were developed for people who share a common health or lifestyle concern. In the comfortable setting of Tucson's Life Enhancement Center, you can give your full attention to your health, lifestyle and education with guidance from some of the country's foremost physicians and researchers. Address issues relative to heart disease, asthma, aging, arthritis, and women's health - and have a great time doing it.

BACK TO TOP

### SPECIAL HEALTH PACKAGES

**LENOX, MASSACHUSETTS**

Canyon Ranch in the Berkshires offers Special Health Packages that are designed to give you the most in-depth exposure to information you need to make lasting changes. Choosing a Special Health Package puts the focus solely on you. An integrated team of health specialists reviews all of the pieces of your wellness profile as a whole and offers advice based on your needs. All packages are customized to you.

BACK TO TOP

You can explore any subject you wish just like turning the pages of a book.

# CHAPTER 2

# Improving Your Health on the Web

Your health is your most valuable asset, and health sites may be the most important sites on the Web. About two-fifths of Internet searches are for medical information.

The Web offers data on almost any ailment. You can learn about your symptoms and various treatments, read case studies of other people who share your ailment, and research the names of experts in your area. Unfortunately, there is no filter to keep out wrong or misleading information. Look for the Health On The Net Foundation. It gives a seal of approval to medical sites. If you take the time and effort to research your condition, you can become an expert on it.

Because so many health-related Web sites are available, it may be hard to choose between them. Information overload can occur easily because of the bulk of material. Fortunately, there are ways to narrow your search. The Health A To Z site can help you find the medical site you want. Other good sites include: Intelihealth; Mental Health Net; IMS-Health (for drug information); Live Healthier, Live Longer (part of the National Institute of Health); Web, MD, former U.S. Surgeon General C. Everett Koop's site (sponsored by Microsoft); and Dr. Dean Edell's site at HealthCentral. Com, Inc. More than four hundred doctors are currently preparing a medical textbook now being published on the Web.

Some of the most popular health sites on the Web are sites about dieting and self-help. Among the dieting sites, the Mayo Clinic, Thrive, and Better Health are popular. Many online self-help groups offer support and treatment information from those who have experienced your condition. They can prevent you from feeling alone. A site like www.canyonranch.com is an example of an interactive health site. The site advertises Canyon Ranch Health Resorts, which are spas located in Tucson, Arizona, and Lenox, Massachusetts. The ranch's experienced team of wellness professionals, ranging from physicians and psychologists to massage, skin care, and fitness experts offers a wide variety of healthy living advice and information via the Internet.

(See www.canyonranch.com Web pages on pages 16–18.) Prescription drug information is available at www.cvsrxnet.com and www.walgreens.com.

Picking a doctor from an HMO list without knowing who can best treat your condition is scary. The good news is that several Websites offer help on picking a doctor. Two such sites are www.certifiedoctor.org and Docboard, which supplies information on credentials and training.

There are two schools of thought regarding the effect of the Web on loneliness and depression. One group is sure that the Web saves people who would not have any human contact without the Web and its chat groups. These include people who live in isolated areas, have unique interests, or are physically unable to get out. Another group suggests that the more time spent on the Web, the more likely the person is to become lonely or depressed. We think both groups have a point — it's good to seek company through the Web, but don't let that prevent you from ever going out of the house again!

Besides using the Web to obtain health information, you can use it to exchange e-mail with your doctor, or to send and receive get-well messages.

One concern with the way the Web operates is that it leaves the blind out of the loop. A number of companies are solving this problem with text-to-speech and speech-to-text software programs. The Lernout and

Hauspie speech product NW is developing this technology with the support of Microsoft and Intel. Dragon Systems Inc. and IBM also offer programs in this area. People who have trouble seeing can enlarge the screens and toolbars on their computers. The www.setisearch.com search engine makes pages easier to read. The www.JFax.com site allows you to hear e-mail.

Some specific examples of sites that provide health-related information follow.

## Pregnancy and Childcare

The World Wide Web has changed forever how expectant parents and parents obtain the information they need about pregnancy and childcare. With four million births a year in the United States alone, this topic obviously has a huge audience! The changing nature of the family — with more single parents and working mothers — has made finding good sources of information more important than ever. Mothers, fathers, and grandparents can use the Web to find information about nannies, daycare, children's sleeping problems, breastfeeding, and even such esoteric subjects as underwater childbirth.

The amount of information on the Web about pregnancy and childbirth is almost overwhelming. For example, Amazon.com lists 2,900 books on pregnancy. The Alta Vista Search site shows 750,430 pages of available information. AOL.com lists the twenty-five most-used sites. They cover virtually every subject one can think of. Here are just a few of the Websites:

- Ask Noah
- Pregnancy Today Online (offers a free weekly newsletter)
- Huggies
- imaternity.com (includes a chat club)
- Babycenter, sponsored by Johnson & Johnson, offers shopping for all your baby needs; chat events; and information about your stage of pregnancy

A few of the childcare sites include:

- NAEYC (The National Association for the Education of Young Children)
- Early Childhood Training Options
- Early Childhood News

## Seniors

The Internet can be a great source of information, entertainment, and companionship for the elderly, who may be prevented by health problems from spending much time away from home. Recognizing the benefits of the Internet, hundreds of nursing homes are installing computers connected to the Internet and hiring computer trainers experienced with elderly users.

The percentage of computer ownership goes down as age goes up. This is partly because the elderly are not as accustomed to using computers. Poor eyesight and age-stressed hands create obstacles for using a computer and reading its screen.

The only solution for overcoming seniors' fear of the computer is to get them to try it. An answer to the vision problem may be Web TV. Since a nineteen-inch or larger television is recommended for use with Web TV, the size of the type and the icons can be much larger on Web TV than on ordinary computer screens. The setup is simple and so is the use. One-third of Web TV customers are over fifty-five.

Good Websites for seniors include:

Senior magazines, such as

- wwws.grandtimes.com/
- www.seniorlivingnewspaper.com/
- www.worldwideseniors.com/
- www.theseniortimes.com

Senior talk:

- www.chatsenior.com/
- www.seniorsite.com/chat/chat1.htm

Senior travel:

- www.elderhostel.org

## Pets

Pets can improve their owners' health because they help them overcome loneliness and depression. But in order for your pet to help you, you have to help your pet stay strong and healthy. In the past, information available outside of a veterinarian's office regarding a pet's health problem was very limited. Today, owners of your pet's same breed will respond to your questions quickly by e-mail. Of course, this does not replace the services of a competent veterinarian.

Web sites addressing the health of pets include:

- www.smart-nutrition.com/pet-health.html
- www.topica.com/read/home.html (for the Virtual Veterinarian newsletter)
- www.aholisticvet.com/main.html
- http://aava.org/pub/aava_front_page.html (for the American Academy of Veterinary Acupuncture)

There are Websites on a wide variety of pet subjects, from products to training to ideas for naming. Many pet owners post pictures and stories about their pets on the Web, and swap information with other pet owners. A number of Websites try to find the owners of lost pets, including www.petloss.com and www.petfinder.org.

## Chapter 2

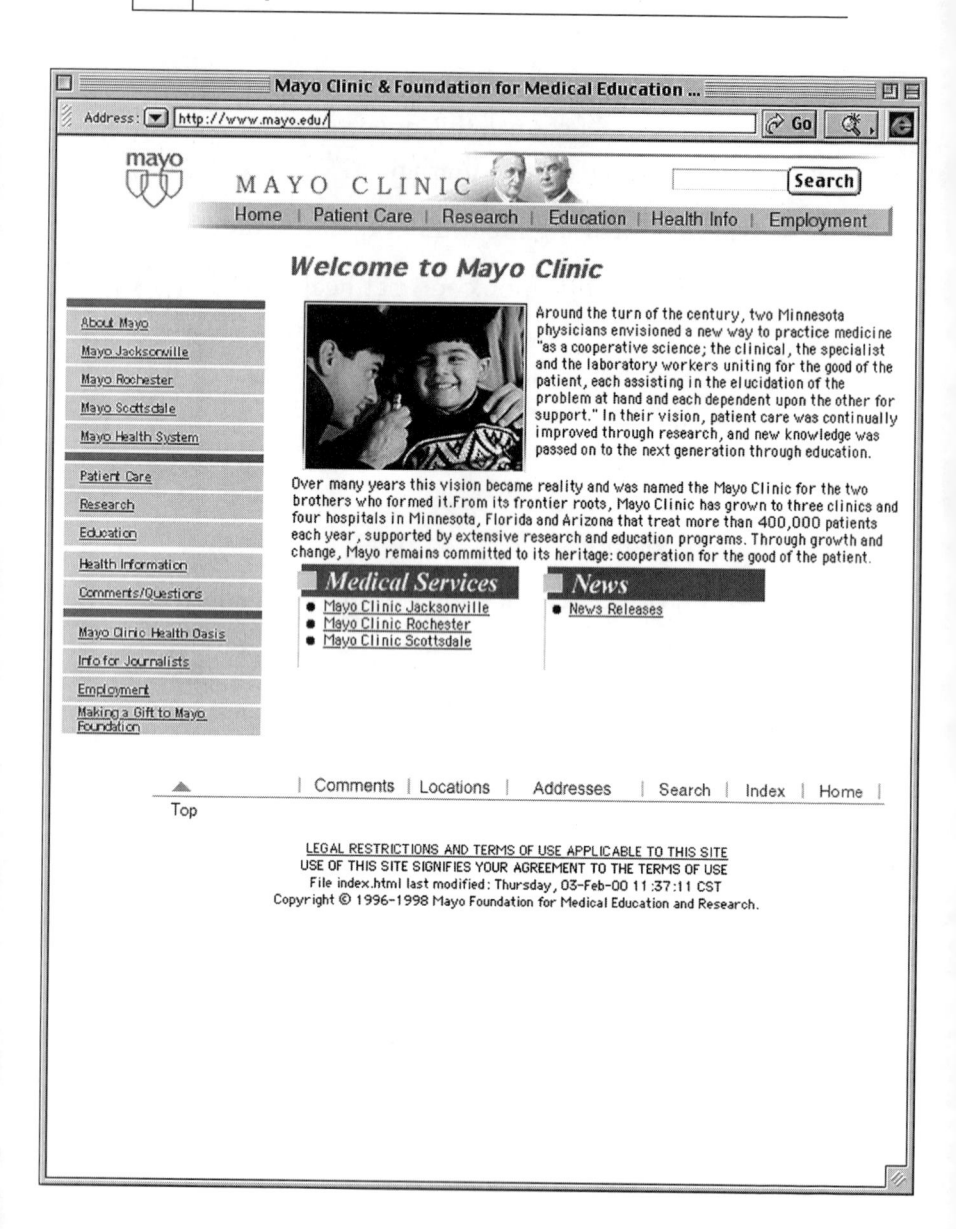

### Welcome to Mayo Clinic

Around the turn of the century, two Minnesota physicians envisioned a new way to practice medicine "as a cooperative science; the clinical, the specialist and the laboratory workers uniting for the good of the patient, each assisting in the elucidation of the problem at hand and each dependent upon the other for support." In their vision, patient care was continually improved through research, and new knowledge was passed on to the next generation through education.

Over many years this vision became reality and was named the Mayo Clinic for the two brothers who formed it. From its frontier roots, Mayo Clinic has grown to three clinics and four hospitals in Minnesota, Florida and Arizona that treat more than 400,000 patients each year, supported by extensive research and education programs. Through growth and change, Mayo remains committed to its heritage: cooperation for the good of the patient.

**Navigation:** Home | Patient Care | Research | Education | Health Info | Employment

**Sidebar:**
- About Mayo
- Mayo Jacksonville
- Mayo Rochester
- Mayo Scottsdale
- Mayo Health System
- Patient Care
- Research
- Education
- Health Information
- Comments/Questions
- Mayo Clinic Health Oasis
- Info for Journalists
- Employment
- Making a Gift to Mayo Foundation

**Medical Services**
- Mayo Clinic Jacksonville
- Mayo Clinic Rochester
- Mayo Clinic Scottsdale

**News**
- News Releases

| Comments | Locations | Addresses | Search | Index | Home |

LEGAL RESTRICTIONS AND TERMS OF USE APPLICABLE TO THIS SITE
USE OF THIS SITE SIGNIFIES YOUR AGREEMENT TO THE TERMS OF USE
File index.html last modified: Thursday, 03-Feb-00 11:37:11 CST
Copyright © 1996-1998 Mayo Foundation for Medical Education and Research.

# Improving Your Health on the Web

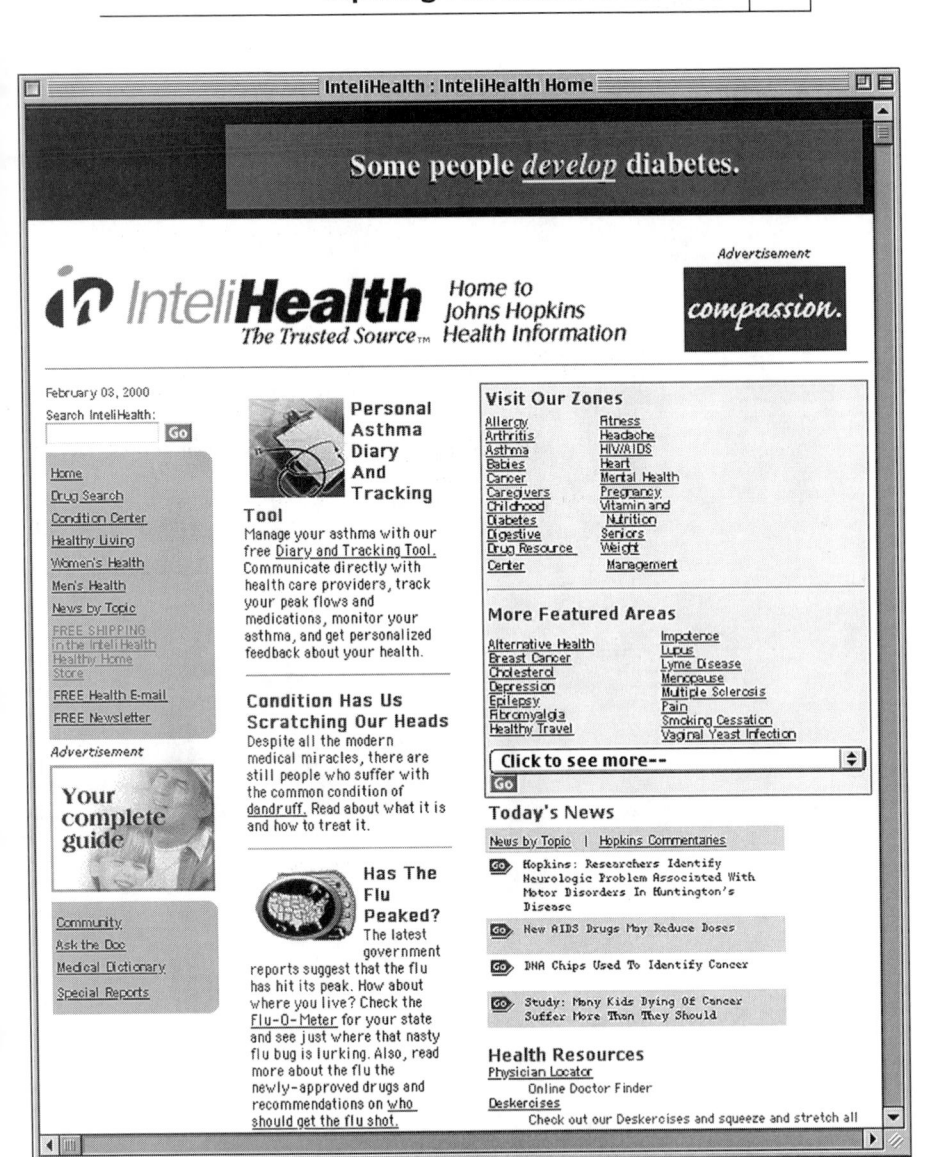

**InteliHealth : InteliHealth Home**

Some people *develop* diabetes.

**InteliHealth** — *The Trusted Source*™
Home to Johns Hopkins Health Information

*Advertisement* — compassion.

February 03, 2000

Search InteliHealth: [ ] Go

- Home
- Drug Search
- Condition Center
- Healthy Living
- Women's Health
- Men's Health
- News by Topic
- FREE SHIPPING in the InteliHealth Healthy Home Store
- FREE Health E-mail
- FREE Newsletter

*Advertisement*
Your complete guide

- Community
- Ask the Doc
- Medical Dictionary
- Special Reports

### Personal Asthma Diary And Tracking Tool

Manage your asthma with our free Diary and Tracking Tool. Communicate directly with health care providers, track your peak flows and medications, monitor your asthma, and get personalized feedback about your health.

### Condition Has Us Scratching Our Heads

Despite all the modern medical miracles, there are still people who suffer with the common condition of dandruff. Read about what it is and how to treat it.

### Has The Flu Peaked?

The latest government reports suggest that the flu has hit its peak. How about where you live? Check the Flu-O-Meter for your state and see just where that nasty flu bug is lurking. Also, read more about the flu the newly-approved drugs and recommendations on who should get the flu shot.

### Visit Our Zones

| | |
|---|---|
| Allergy | Fitness |
| Arthritis | Headache |
| Asthma | HIV/AIDS |
| Babies | Heart |
| Cancer | Mental Health |
| Caregivers | Pregnancy |
| Childhood | Vitamin and Nutrition |
| Diabetes | Seniors |
| Digestive | Weight |
| Drug Resource Center | Management |

### More Featured Areas

| | |
|---|---|
| Alternative Health | Impotence |
| Breast Cancer | Lupus |
| Cholesterol | Lyme Disease |
| Depression | Menopause |
| Epilepsy | Multiple Sclerosis |
| Fibromyalgia | Pain |
| Healthy Travel | Smoking Cessation |
| | Vaginal Yeast Infection |

[ Click to see more-- ▼ ]
Go

### Today's News

News by Topic | Hopkins Commentaries

- ▶ Hopkins: Researchers Identify Neurologic Problem Associated With Motor Disorders In Huntington's Disease
- ▶ New AIDS Drugs May Reduce Doses
- ▶ DNA Chips Used To Identify Cancer
- ▶ Study: Many Kids Dying Of Cancer Suffer More Than They Should

### Health Resources

Physician Locator
  Online Doctor Finder
Deskercises
  Check out our Deskercises and squeeze and stretch all

**28** | **Chapter 2**

---

NOAH: New York Online Access to Health Home Page

Address: http://www.noah.cuny.edu/

*NOAH: New York Online Access to Health*

Welcome
Bienvenido(a)

Health Topics
Word Search
NOAH Providers
What's New
Help
About NOAH
Feedback
NOAH Sponsors

Temas de Salud
Búsqueda por Palabras
Proveedores de NOAH
Lo Nuevo
Ayuda
Acerca de NOAH
Comentarios
Patrocinadores

NYAM   NYPL   NYPL

Awards   Premios

*InfoTrac Health Reference Gold*

*Pregúntale a NOAH sobre la salud*

---

### NOAH: New York Online Access to Health

[Welcome]
[Health Topics] [Word Search] [NOAH Providers] [What's New] [Help] [NYAM] [NYPL] [About NOAH] [Feedback] [NOAH Sponsors] [Infotrac Health Reference Center Gold]

### Pregúntale a NOAH Sobre la Salud

[Bienvenido(a)]
[Temas de Salud] [Búsquedas Por Palabras] [Proveedores de NOAH] [Lo Nuevo]
[Ayuda] [Biblioteca Pública de Nueva York (NYPL)]
[Acerca de NOAH] [Comentarios] [Patrocinadores de NOAH]

# CHAPTER 3

## Buying on the Web

The Internet provides new ways to maximize the value of your money. You can acquire products more cheaply, sell things you don't need, and make wiser investments.

Person-to-person selling of goods and services started online in 1997 and developed into a giant complex of new groups posting thousands of orders on bulletin boards. Suppose you want to buy a recreational sailboat — a search engine can help you. Typing in "recreational sailboats" on AOL.comSearch brought up 480 different sites. You can then narrow your search to the specific type of boat you are looking for, and find a seller. Groups are divided into tight segments in order to reduce the number of pages you need to search in looking for an item.

Other sites that allow you to buy on the Web include Buy.com, Shopnow.com, and eBay.

Buy.com guarantees the lowest price. It owns over three thousand Web addresses — including Buy Music.com, Buy Games.com, and Buy Comp.com — and intends to offer the lowest price in every product category in which it competes. Through a unique tracking and search system it combs competitors' computer price lists (using a variety of company names) to determine the lowest prices. Buy.com then uses this information to offer the item at a lower price. Buy.com expects sales of hundreds of millions of dollars per year.

Shopnow.com offers products from more than 29,000 brand names and specialty shops. Type in what you want, and Shopnow will find it online.

Collectors spend billions of dollars every year at auctions and flea markets. If you like antiques but don't want to spend every rainy Saturday hiking through the county flea markets, there are now more than one hundred auction sites. The biggest site is eBay, which runs an online national auction. Bidders submit their offers and eBay processes them, though it doesn't own any of the products offered. More than seven hundred thousand items may be featured at any one time. Collectors of anything — from Barbie dolls to old bottles — list themselves on the classified pages and billboards with other collectors. eBay is also opening regional auction sites that will compete with local classified advertising.

Car buyers can access dealer invoices from Carpoint and Autobytel.com to help them negotiate prices with car dealers.

Priceline.com offers to find services and products at the price you want to pay.

Escrow services are systematic ways to describe items and clear delivery times. Thus the item and the payment are held by a third party who guarantees the transfer.

Wal-Mart, the world's largest retailer, has established a site called Wal-Mart Online. This site offers a wide variety of products including toys, sporting goods, home appliances, electronics, and books, as well as links to Wal-Mart's customer service, stores, and special parts of the company like the Wal-Mart Foundation and Sam's Club.

AT&T's One Net Service site offers information for home and business. It has an online catalog, online customer service, a market square for shopping, communication tools, and maps. AT&T networking offers a whole means of doing business on the go.

Allstate, one of the largest insurers of autos and homes, has recently decided to join the Internet. Previously, it sold insurance only through agents. Now, in a competitive move, it will pay agents a reduced commission for policies sold in their territory over the Internet. Allstate found a way to manage one of today's most difficult problems — maintaining its current system of distribution while competing with companies that sell on the Internet.

You can even buy or sell a company over the Web. MergerNetwork.com lists thousands of businesses for sale.

With all the products to choose from on the Web, some consumers don't feel comfortable shopping there. Surveys of Web retailers indicate that most shoppers who select items give up at the checkout. They don't buy because it's not always easy to pay. Amazon developed a care-click system that keeps your credit information on file so that it can bring it up on all future purchases. AOL offers quick checkout, Yahoo! Inc. offers Yahoo! Shopping, and Excite Inc. offers express order services. Some U.S. and international banks are developing smart cards or certificates of authority to aid Internet commerce.

Some specific examples of businesses on the Web follow.

## Amazon.com

Amazon makes book buying easy — you can buy a book with a single click. This company makes it easy to search for any book by simply typing in the subject matter, title, or author.

To what can we attribute Amazon's great success? First, it's a personalized service. It has a unique computerized system that recommends other books in the same pattern as those you've already purchased. It's like having your own personal salesperson who knows what you like and calls you when a new book you'd enjoy is available.

Amazon lists three million books, but stocks only three hundred thousand. The rest must come in from the distributor and then be shipped by Amazon. However, the speed of the operation is such that, with three distribution points, books often can be shipped the same day a shopper places an order.

Amazon.com now allows other companies to list their products on its Website. A company or individual can list up to three thousand products at a cost of $9.95 per month plus a percent of sales. This will add approximately five hundred thousand products to Amazon's site. There soon may not be much Amazon doesn't sell, since the company has begun offering toys, health supplies, apparel, magazines, videos, and music CDs — and more products are on the way.

Amazon is currently the biggest consumer merchant on the Web, with projected year 2000 sales of $2.3 billion dollars. Most of their customers are repeat customers, perhaps because consumers feel secure in placing an order. They have confidence that the orders will be received, that the credit card purchase will be properly handled, and that they will receive their purchases in a reasonable period of time.

Books are the top-selling products on the Web, with fourteen thousand Web booksellers in the United States alone. Competition from other booksellers may become tougher in the future. For example, Borders has merged with Bertelsmann to form a global book company. The global book market is estimated at eighty billion dollars yearly. In order to compete with Amazon, Books-A-Million has added a Website to assist its 172 bookstores.

One unique book site is called Book Tech. It prints sections of books for classroom use based on a table of contents prepared by the instructor. Varsity Book.com offers textbooks on the Web at discount prices, and with the convenience of not having to wait in the school bookstore line.

Electronic books and online libraries also add to the mix. Among the other interesting, book-related sites are antique book sites and the Library of Congress Website.

Literary events are listed on the Web, often advertising authors reading selections from their work.

## Victoria's Secret

Victoria's Secret, a woman's clothing retailer, created an advertising campaign that resulted in tens of millions of hits on its Website. (A hit is a connection to the site from another computer — probably a potential customer.)

The campaign started with publicity about its upcoming ad, timed to air during the Super Bowl. The Super Bowl ad touted a Victoria's Secret fashion show coming to the Web that Wednesday evening. The show featured twenty of the world's most beautiful women wearing Victoria's Secret garments.

Two million visitors turned on the fashion show. Many saw only snow on their screens because of technology problems. Yet the campaign was a huge sales success. We can expect to see many more major advertisers combine TV, newspapers, radio, and the Web to create excitement for their products.

## Shoes

Shoes have joined the Web. Shoe sizes rarely change, and many shoppers want to buy the same brand and style they have always bought in the past. In many places the availability of special sizes and styles is limited, as is the availability of special shoes for various activities such as nursing and construction work. The Web offers many sites that make a wide selection of shoe sizes and styles possible. Sites include:

- Nordstroms.com
- ShoesOnTheNet.com
- Zappos.com
- Webbedfoot.com

## Banks

Banks are rolling out their Web systems, offering paperless transactions.

For many banks, developing Internet services is much cheaper than opening branch offices. Not being tied to brick and mortar is important as neighborhoods change. New changes in the bank, insurance, and investment laws will encourage one-stop banking, allowing you to pay bills, review your account activity, transfer funds, and stop payment on a check, all online. Among the banks offering Web services are The Bank of Montreal, Harris Bank, Royal Bank of Canada, Canadian Imperial Bank of Commerce, and Bank One.

## Freebies

There are thousands of "freebies" offered on the Web. Websites offer a variety of things for free and usually rely on advertising to pay the way.

Here is a partial list of the most-visited sites:

- LinksandMore.com offers free software, graphics, screensavers, fonts, e-mail, digital postcards, games, and music;
- A1Clipart.com features one thousand free images;
- Oracletree.com offers free astrology materials, herbal and botanical supplies, catalogs, publications, and "kindness cards";
- Blue Mountain Arts personalizes and sends online greeting cards for free;
- Lilli.Clara.Net/Free Saver/New 1.htm offers thousands of free screensavers;
- SmartShop1.com offers thousands of free catalogs and magazines;

- eTour.com finds the best sites for your interests and brings them to your screen;
- Arcadepod.com offers three-dimensional games, board games, and online casinos;
- Business.Fortunecity.com offers forms for receiving rebates and free goods. Hundreds of items are listed. The site also offers to mail hundreds of coupons to you for a two-dollar charge.

## Chapter 3

### eToys - Where great ideas come to you!

Address: http://www.etoys.com/html/et_home.shtml?rsrc=ident&SID=a884084318207615

# eToys.com
**Where great ideas come to you.™**

- home
- help
- my eToys
- shopping cart

TOYS | BABY STORE | BOOKS | SOFT WARE | VIDEOS | MUSIC | VIDEO GAMES

toysearch | shop by age | toy recommendations | toy brands | toy categories

### welcome
February 3, 2000

**2 WAYS TO SEARCH**

**quicksearch**
[go]

**toysearch™**
search by age, category, and price!

**shop eToys by age**
- 0-12 months
- 1 year
- 2 years
- 3 years
- 4 years
- 5 years
- 6 years
- 7 years
- 8 years
- 9-12 years

**toy recommendations**
- Bestsellers
- Fantastic Finds
- 200 under $20
- Award Winners
- Toys for Special Needs
- From the Movies
- Popular Characters
- Classic Toys
- Sales & Savings
- Feature Shops
- Last-Minute Gifts

**ideas & activities**
- Idea Center
- Oppenheim Activities
- Rosie's Readers

**toy categories**
- Action Figures
- Arts & Crafts
- Construction
- Dolls
- Games
- Learning
- Make-Believe
- Radio Control
- Stuffed Toys
- See 40 More...

**toy brands**
Well-known Brands:
- Barbie
- Erector
- Estes
- Fisher-Price
- LEGO
- See 75 More...

Specialty Brands:
- Breyer
- BRIO
- Discovery Toys
- Eden
- Lamaze
- See 75 More...

**gift services**
- Gift Center
- Gift Certificates
- Create a Gift Registry
- Find a Gift Registry
- Birthday Reminders
- Gift Wrapping
- Wish List

**eToys newsletter**
Our newsletter has great ideas for kids and updates on new features at eToys. Sign up!

### 50 of our favorite games
- Family Games
- Party Games
- Preschool Games
- School-Age Games

From Twister to Yahtzee, we've got great games for the whole family.

### the hobby shop
Looking to build a model? The eToys Hobby Shop has a ton of kits, plus plenty of tips to get you started.

### pre-order at eToys!
Anakin, Jar Jar, and Darth Maul are back. Star Wars: Episode I is just one of our upcoming video releases you can order now.

### for kids who love...
...dolls, there's no place more divine than our Doll Boutique. See other Feature Shops for more to spark kids' passions.

Shopping at eToys is 100% safe - **guaranteed**

**FOR FEBRUARY...**

**fantastic finds**
Come take a look at the best toys you've never heard of.

**200 treasures under $20**
Who says fun has to be expensive? We've found 200 wonderful toys under $20.

**BESTSELLERS**
- Books
- Software

---

© eToys Inc. 2000 All rights reserved. EToys® is a registered trademark of eToys Inc.

# Buying on the Web 39

## Welcome to e-centives!

Address: http://www.e-centives.com/servlet/product/ehtml/signup/esid+ECE-2GA3XB00C4TPEQTE-1

sign-up | e-centives privacy | partner stores | help

## free special offers & digital coupons!

e-centives™ — what you want

**e-centives** [E-'sent-tivs] n.

Special online offers and digital coupons tailored to your unique shopping interests -- ready to redeem when you're ready to shop!

**get what you want**

- **FREE** special offers from your favorite brands
- **FREE** organizer--conveniently stores your e-centives online
- **Choose** to receive e-centives via e-mail
- **Private**--Your information is safeguarded for privacy

**already a member?** [members login here]

### sign up & save!
Enter your e-mail address, password and choose your shopping interests.

e-mail:
[          ]
password:
[          ]
re-enter password:
[          ]

**Your shopping interests:**

- ☐ Automotive
- ☐ Baby Stuff
- ☐ Books & Magazines
- ☐ Computers
- ☐ Electronics
- ☐ Fashion
- ☐ Gifts & Gourmet
- ☐ Groceries
- ☐ Health & Beauty
- ☐ Hobbies
- ☐ Home & Gardening
- ☐ Local
- ☐ Music & Video
- ☐ Pets
- ☐ Services
- ☐ Sports & Fitness
- ☐ Toys & Games
- ☐ Travel

[sign me up!]

your privacy is safeguarded          need more info

By signing up for e-centives you acknowledge that you have read and agree to our terms of service.

**reviewed by TRUST-e**
site privacy statement
Trust-e click to verify

**40** Chapter 3

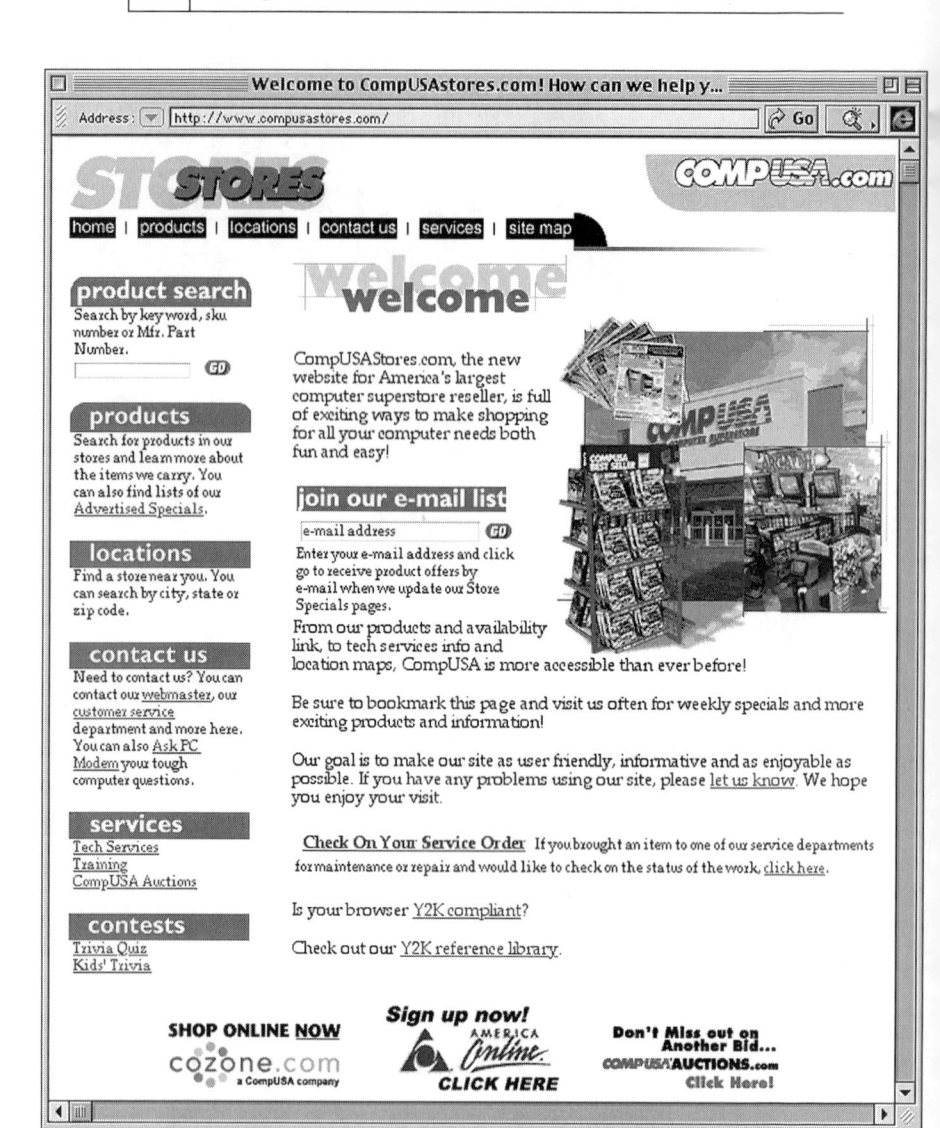

---

## Welcome to CompUSAstores.com! How can we help y...

Address: http://www.compusastores.com/

### STORES | COMPUSA.com

home | products | locations | contact us | services | site map

**product search**
Search by key word, sku number or Mfr. Part Number.

**products**
Search for products in our stores and learn more about the items we carry. You can also find lists of our Advertised Specials.

**locations**
Find a store near you. You can search by city, state or zip code.

**contact us**
Need to contact us? You can contact our webmaster, our customer service department and more here. You can also Ask PC Modem your tough computer questions.

**services**
Tech Services
Training
CompUSA Auctions

**contests**
Trivia Quiz
Kids' Trivia

## welcome

CompUSAStores.com, the new website for America's largest computer superstore reseller, is full of exciting ways to make shopping for all your computer needs both fun and easy!

### join our e-mail list
e-mail address

Enter your e-mail address and click go to receive product offers by e-mail when we update our Store Specials pages.

From our products and availability link, to tech services info and location maps, CompUSA is more accessible than ever before!

Be sure to bookmark this page and visit us often for weekly specials and more exciting products and information!

Our goal is to make our site as user friendly, informative and as enjoyable as possible. If you have any problems using our site, please let us know. We hope you enjoy your visit.

**Check On Your Service Order** If you brought an item to one of our service departments for maintenance or repair and would like to check on the status of the work, click here.

Is your browser Y2K compliant?

Check out our Y2K reference library.

---

**SHOP ONLINE NOW**
cozone.com
a CompUSA company

**Sign up now!**
AMERICA Online
**CLICK HERE**

**Don't Miss out on Another Bid...**
COMPUSA AUCTIONS.com
**Click Here!**

# CHAPTER 4

## Selling on the Web

Why should a company be on the World Wide Web now? Today's fast-paced information and technology age has increasingly impatient consumers — not willing to wait long to fill their needs and wants. "I want it now" is the catchphrase of the day. Time is critical.

A company must take advantage of this new attitude with a site on the World Wide Web. When a company places an advertisement in a magazine, newspaper, or on TV, people reading the publication or watching the station will see their advertisement. If a company includes its Web address on a television or newspaper advertisement, it can immediately win the business of people who are interested in their product. People can easily visit the site to find exactly what they want in the fastest and most effective way, and order it.

A company's Website can combine full-color graphics, text, video, and sound to effectively market its material to consumers twenty-four hours a day, seven days a week. The site can give answers to the most frequently asked questions (called FAQs in Internet lingo).

Want to start your own Web page? Companies can be on the Web for small investments of as little as twenty dollars per month. The potential audience is more than one hundred million people. A World Wide Web presence immediately opens new avenues, brings in new customers, and introduces new markets to the audience. It puts business information, catalogs, products, demos, and services into the hands of consumers within seconds without paper costs, postage costs, or the hiring of an expensive fulfillment staff. It also eliminates the high costs and space and creative limitations that go along with conventional advertising. The lower cost of transactions on the Web is causing many companies and industries to evaluate how they can save by using the Web for their sales, purchases, and for supplying information. A retailer can also do low-cost market research on the Web both by answering consumers' questions and asking them questions about their needs. Offering free information is also a good way to attract people to your Website. An example would be an insurance company offering free information on how to prolong your life.

The Web has changed consumer ideas about price comparison, shopping convenience, speed, and service. As of this writing, one quarter of Americans connects to the Web every day — many from work. No one wants to wait and no one wants to be cut off. Considering the large audience your site may attract, you may want to ask yourself whether your company is ready to handle the traffic. If not, look to outsourcing. Nothing angers a customer more than not getting a timely response to an inquiry.

We will discuss advertising on the Web in more detail in Chapter 8.

## Website Hosting

A new industry has developed to service businesses on the Web. Want to start a business? Want to promote a business you already have? Want to share your collection, trade, or talk about your hobby? Having your own Web page is a great way to accomplish these goals. The American Management Association offers one-day seminars on "The Basics of Website Design" in cities all across the country. The seminars teach you how to select a service provider, choose a site, design and update a Web page, handle security concerns, and advertise on the Web. Another option for learning how to design a Web page is a new software package called the Complete Web Studio 20, which makes designing a Web page easy. You also can learn how to develop a Web site using software from Go Daddy at http://www.godaddy.com.

Priced from twenty dollars a month, a variety of companies provide Web hosting services. These services include domain name registration, e-mail forwarding, credit card services, and e-mail response.

## e-Web

The e-Web is the part of the Web accessible by e-mail, rather than through search engines. Ray Tomlin invented e-mail so he could communicate with other engineers while working on a government contract. It has changed the way America does business and the way families and friends communicate.

Once it expanded past Tomlin and his fellow engineers, e-mail was first widely used for business communications. Most e-commerce — eighty percent at this writing — is still business to business, with IBM the leader in developing business systems. Since e-mail can live forever in a system servicer or in taped storage, businesses now need to develop policies on how to control employee e-mail and the destruction of e-mail files.

E-mail has expanded outside of business to become a part of everyday life. Old friendships, long abandoned because of a reluctance to write letters, have been given new life by the ease of e-mail. There are tens of millions of e-mail accounts in the U.S. alone.

The following e-sites are keyed to consumers:

- estamp delivers postage on AOL so you can download it onto envelopes;

- eThe People connects to local, state, and federal officials;
- eStyle plans to offer female-oriented sites starting with Babystyle.com;
- eBay is the largest person-to-person auction site connecting approximately four million buyers and services;
- eToys offers more than 750 brands;
- www.ecentives.com offers electronic coupons, discounts, and special offers, sent to your own ecentives page.

E-stamp gets USPS approval to print stamps on the Web.

# Chapter 4

### DOCKSIDE REALTY INC. presents

## Sarasota and her beautiful Islands (Longboat Key, Siesta Key, Bird Key and Lido Key)

**Tangerine Bay**

**Turtle Rock**

**Pelican Cove**

- Home Page
- Tangerine Bay Club
- Turtle Rock
- The Boathouse
- mailform
- White Meadow Lake

Please join us on a "tour" of the many facets of this casual, yet sophisticated, community by the sea ...

Experience our lifestyles; visit our homes and our beaches; see our theatres, our symphony and the opera house; share our community resources - schools, colleges and universities; our modern hospitals; our parks - the new library; Play our golf courses and tennis courts, and sail and fish our spectacular bay; Live your dreams every day!

Sarasota? - you'll love her! To learn how you can enjoy our wonderful way of life call our office today and let one of our friendly associates help you find the "lifestyle" that is perfect for you.

Local business uses the Web to sell real estate and boat storage.

Selling on the Web    47

## The Boathouse

### World class High and Dry Boat Storage

THE BOATHOUSE ON LONGBOAT is Florida's finest enclosed boat storage facility. 194 boats are sheltered in a "state of the art" environment designed to the most rigid specifications. Over 15 years of, practical "hands on", marina experience were merged with the latest in storage, launch and retrieval technologies to create the BOATHOUSE. The result is a design created to give your *boat* the very best protection available and to give *you*, the boat owner, the most efficient, courteous, and convenient "in and out" service possible.

Home Page
Tangerine Bay Club
Turtle Rock
The Boathouse
mailform
White Meadow Lake

The main building is a modern steel structure capable of withstanding hurricane force winds. Oversized structural members have all been "hot dip" galvanized to prevent the rust and corrosion so common to waterfront structures. Currently available storage spaces accommodate boats up to 32 feet in overall length, up to 10'4" in height, and up to 8'6" beam. The unique louvered design of the BOATHOUSE provides important mildew fighting ventilation while it keeps the boats sheltered from the sun, wind and rain. Tucked away from the elements, your boat's teak, vinyl, fiberglass and canvas will stay "like new." This will enhance your boating pleasure while it preserves the value of your boating investment.

## Chapter 4

KM.net makes selling on the Web easy! Open a business at this mall and they help you get started.

# CHAPTER 5

## Investing on the Web

Stock trading on the Internet has become big business. Web traders deal in Internet stocks and all other stocks and bonds. Online trading doubled in 1997 and 1998, as people discovered that they could trade anywhere, twenty-four hours a day. As of this writing, one quarter of all trades were made on the Web. Investors who trade on the Web trade approximately twenty times as often as other traders annually. Currently, approximately ten million households are using the Web for investing or research. According to research by Joe Ricketts, chairman of Ameritrade Holdings, most online traders are not desperate gamblers out for easy money, but wealthy and well-educated individuals. About a third of all online traders manage more than $250,000 in investments.

There are several popular trading sites, including:

- Ameritrade
- Charles Schwab & Co.
- E-Trade
- Merrill Lynch & Co.
- Morgan Stanley Dean Witter & Co.

Of the more than eighty online brokers, Schwab is number one, trading three billion dollars in online securities weekly — about a third of all total trades. Schwab charges a flat fee of about thirty dollars for most transactions. Its online trades equal more than half its total volume. Customers like its smooth handling, help, and advice. The broker also has an after-hours session.

E-Trade advertises round-the-clock trading as low as $14.95 per trade at its one-stop financial center. You can invest in stocks, options, and four thousand mutual funds. Another popular site is Stockmaster, which gets up to one million hits each day.

Online discussion groups make trading fun. When you can talk about your trades, they become more intense. Of course, this also makes it easy to receive misinformation. Mutual fund bulletin boards and chat groups exist on many sites. The oldest chat group is www.DEJA.com; www.Fundalarm.com carries many critical comments about funds; and www.Brill.com is a hangout for mutual fund investors.

Direct stock purchase plans allow customers to buy without brokers' fees. More than five hundred companies offer stock plans, which they say also tends to make customers loyal to their goods and services. Brokers' sites offer sources of stock information. Among the more popular Websites for stock research are:

- Morningstar
- Bloomberg
- Quicken
- Mutual Pool
- Smart Money
- E-Trade
- J. P. Morgan

If you are considering investing in a company's stock, the company's prospectus is usually available instantly on the Web. Remember that an investor, like any shopper, should be on the lookout for scams.

Besides stocks for American companies, investors can also consider American depository receipts, which are foreign stocks traded on American exchanges.

But investing can involve more than just stocks. Among the Internet mutual funds are CMGI and Internet Capital Group, Inc.

A new Website has eliminated much of the mystery of bond trading. The Bond Marketing Association posts daily prices, yields, and credit ratings. One promising investment opportunity is municipal bonds, of which there are more than one million outstanding issues. Municipal bonds are tax free and can yield more income than treasuries.

## Valuing Internet Stocks

The Internet has changed everything in the stock market. Studies show that individual trading on the Internet grows by the thousands every day. What will happen when fifty million people in India, a hundred million people in China, and another hundred million in South America start to trade? Overload! Technology will need to address how to handle the increasing number of stock traders on the Internet.

Internet stocks do not behave like ordinary stocks. Day traders have found that the stocks can fall or rise thirty points on any given day. Famous investor Warren Buffet suggests a course in valuing Internet stocks which would fail any student who tried to assign a value to an Internet stock. Amazon.com has proven that the more it loses, the more valuable its stock becomes. There are no fundamentals. Price to earnings ratios are impossible because there are no earnings. Amazon says its profits may not come from books but from all the other products and advertising it sells.

The oddity of Internet stocks has led to the development of a new valuation approach called EVA (Economic Value Added). The theory behind EVA is that future growth value compared to cost of capital will determine worth. For example, Amazon would need an average growth rate of about sixty percent, with sales of sixty-three billion dollars in ten years. Yet total book sales are only estimated to be sixteen billion dollars in ten years. The value must come from the other products and the advertising it sells.

Here are some other examples of how Internet stock growth will create an economic world. Yahoo shares increased seventy-five percent in thirteen days. Books-A-Million stock went from four dollars to thirty-nine dollars in two days. And On-Sale Inc. went up sixty-three percent in a single day. But traffic, stickiness, watches, hits, and even sales volume do not necessarily equal profits or a good return on investment.

Federal Reserve Board Chairman Alan Greenspan compared the Internet stock mania to the lottery. There will be a few big winners, and many losers.

## IPOs

An Initial Public Offering or IPO is a company's first offering of its stock to the public. IPOs are the stuff dreams are made of — a way to become ultra-rich through technology. The Internet has made possible the sale of IPOs without the help of investment bankers. The Securities and Exchange Commission has issued rules on offering securities on the Internet. IPO shares can be traded on www.witcapital.com.

It takes a leap of faith to buy IPOs on the belief that stocks only go up. When will the bubble burst? When will the market collapse? What will end the wild speculation? No one wants the party to end, so they keep buying.

But there is a general consensus that the market is over-priced and that there will be an eventual decline in the market. As the stock market has fluctuated, prices of many Internet stocks fell fifty percent from their high. Many are now below their initial offering prices.

If you want to try trading on the stock market, it is important to understand how to make money both when stocks go up and when stocks go down. The mistake people make is thinking that they can only make money when a stock goes up. Knowledgeable traders will make money whether the market goes up or down.

# Investing on the Web 55

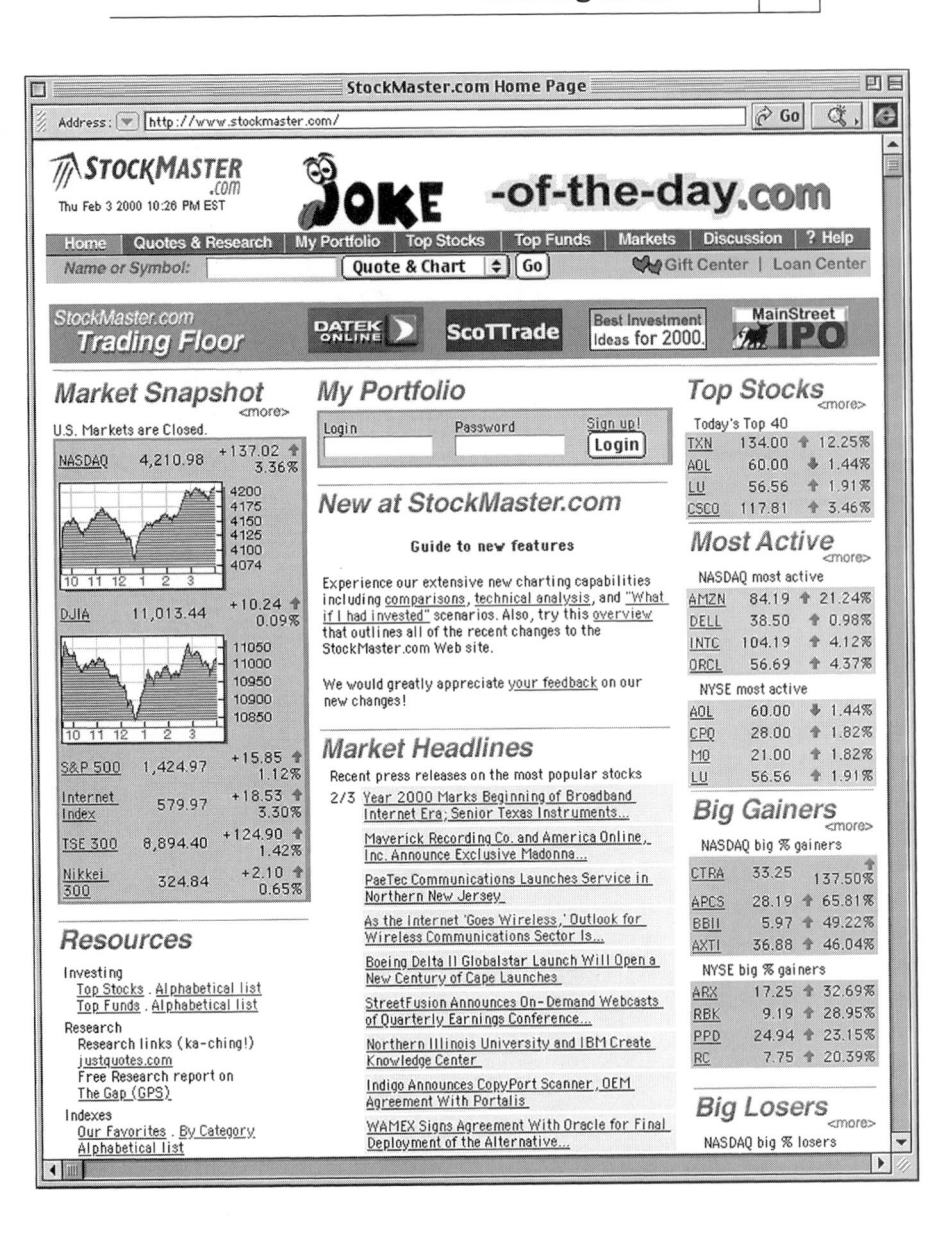

## StockMaster.com Home Page

Address: http://www.stockmaster.com/

**STOCKMASTER.com**
Thu Feb 3 2000 10:26 PM EST

**JOKE-of-the-day.com**

| Home | Quotes & Research | My Portfolio | Top Stocks | Top Funds | Markets | Discussion | ? Help |

Name or Symbol: [    ]   Quote & Chart [Go]   Gift Center | Loan Center

**StockMaster.com Trading Floor** — DATEK ONLINE — ScoTTrade — Best Investment Ideas for 2000. — MainStreet IPO

### Market Snapshot <more>
U.S. Markets are Closed.

| NASDAQ | 4,210.98 | +137.02 ↑ 3.36% |
|---|---|---|

(chart: 4200, 4175, 4150, 4125, 4100, 4074)
10 11 12 1 2 3

| DJIA | 11,013.44 | +10.24 ↑ 0.09% |
|---|---|---|

(chart: 11050, 11000, 10950, 10900, 10850)
10 11 12 1 2 3

| S&P 500 | 1,424.97 | +15.85 ↑ 1.12% |
| Internet Index | 579.97 | +18.53 ↑ 3.30% |
| TSE 300 | 8,894.40 | +124.90 ↑ 1.42% |
| Nikkei 300 | 324.84 | +2.10 ↑ 0.65% |

### Resources
Investing
  Top Stocks . Alphabetical list
  Top Funds . Alphabetical list
Research
  Research links (ka-ching!)
  justquotes.com
  Free Research report on
  The Gap (GPS)
Indexes
  Our Favorites . By Category
  Alphabetical list

### My Portfolio
Login [    ]   Password [    ]   Sign up!  [Login]

### New at StockMaster.com

**Guide to new features**

Experience our extensive new charting capabilities including comparisons, technical analysis, and "What if I had invested" scenarios. Also, try this overview that outlines all of the recent changes to the StockMaster.com Web site.

We would greatly appreciate your feedback on our new changes!

### Market Headlines
Recent press releases on the most popular stocks
2/3 Year 2000 Marks Beginning of Broadband Internet Era; Senior Texas Instruments...
Maverick Recording Co. and America Online, Inc. Announce Exclusive Madonna...
PaeTec Communications Launches Service in Northern New Jersey
As the Internet 'Goes Wireless,' Outlook for Wireless Communications Sector Is...
Boeing Delta II Globalstar Launch Will Open a New Century of Cape Launches
StreetFusion Announces On-Demand Webcasts of Quarterly Earnings Conference...
Northern Illinois University and IBM Create Knowledge Center
Indigo Announces CopyPort Scanner, OEM Agreement With Portalis
WAMEX Signs Agreement With Oracle for Final Deployment of the Alternative...

### Top Stocks <more>
Today's Top 40
| TXN | 134.00 ↑ 12.25% |
| AOL | 60.00 ↓ 1.44% |
| LU | 56.56 ↑ 1.91% |
| CSCO | 117.81 ↑ 3.46% |

### Most Active <more>
NASDAQ most active
| AMZN | 84.19 ↑ 21.24% |
| DELL | 38.50 ↑ 0.98% |
| INTC | 104.19 ↑ 4.12% |
| ORCL | 56.69 ↑ 4.37% |

NYSE most active
| AOL | 60.00 ↓ 1.44% |
| CPQ | 28.00 ↑ 1.82% |
| MO | 21.00 ↑ 1.82% |
| LU | 56.56 ↑ 1.91% |

### Big Gainers <more>
NASDAQ big % gainers
| CTRA | 33.25 ↑ 137.50% |
| APCS | 28.19 ↑ 65.81% |
| BBII | 5.97 ↑ 49.22% |
| AXTI | 36.88 ↑ 46.04% |

NYSE big % gainers
| ARX | 17.25 ↑ 32.69% |
| RBK | 9.19 ↑ 28.95% |
| PPD | 24.94 ↑ 23.15% |
| RC | 7.75 ↑ 20.39% |

### Big Losers <more>
NASDAQ big % losers

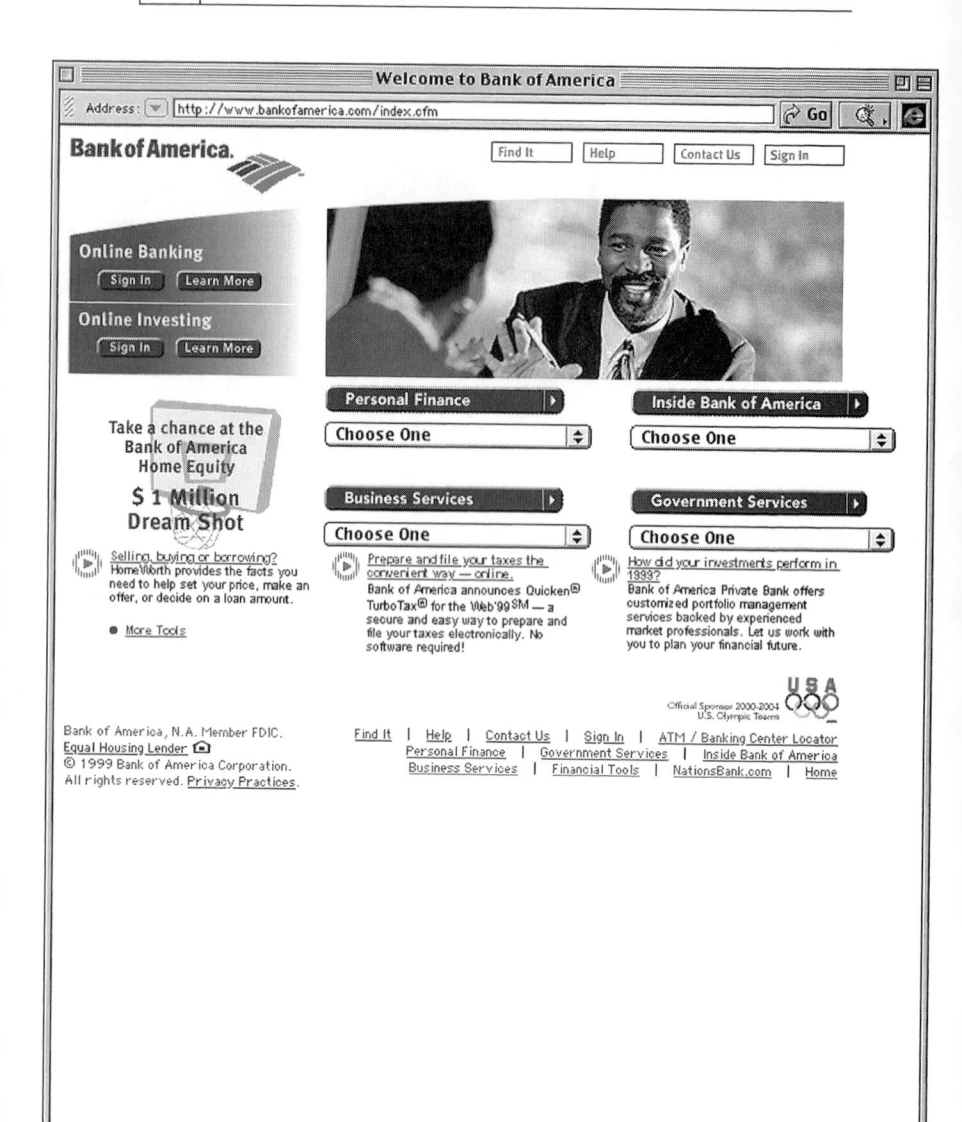

# Chapter 5

---

**Welcome to Bank of America**

Address: http://www.bankofamerica.com/index.cfm

**Bank of America.**

Find It | Help | Contact Us | Sign In

**Online Banking**
Sign In | Learn More

**Online Investing**
Sign In | Learn More

Take a chance at the Bank of America Home Equity **$1 Million Dream Shot**

Selling, buying or borrowing? HomeWorth provides the facts you need to help set your price, make an offer, or decide on a loan amount.

- More Tools

**Personal Finance**
Choose One

**Business Services**
Choose One

Prepare and file your taxes the convenient way — online.
Bank of America announces Quicken® TurboTax® for the Web'99 SM — a secure and easy way to prepare and file your taxes electronically. No software required!

**Inside Bank of America**
Choose One

**Government Services**
Choose One

How did your investments perform in 1998?
Bank of America Private Bank offers customized portfolio management services backed by experienced market professionals. Let us work with you to plan your financial future.

Official Sponsor 2000-2004
U.S. Olympic Teams

Bank of America, N.A. Member FDIC.
Equal Housing Lender
© 1999 Bank of America Corporation.
All rights reserved. Privacy Practices.

Find It | Help | Contact Us | Sign In | ATM / Banking Center Locator
Personal Finance | Government Services | Inside Bank of America
Business Services | Financial Tools | NationsBank.com | Home

# CHAPTER 6

## Security on the Web

Security is the foremost issue that will affect success of business and personal use of the Internet.

Three significant issues to consider are:

1. Protecting your wallet
2. Protecting personal data
3. Protecting children

### Protecting Your Wallet

Some retailers on the Web expect you to have the faith of a child. They ask you, in effect, "Just give me your credit card number, expiration date, Social Security number, and driver's license number. Trust me. I'll ship what you ordered. I promise!"

A smart consumer who isn't familiar with the Web retailer may reasonably respond: "No thanks. I don't know you and I don't feel secure."

Researchers say that Internet users want a sign of assurance for Web products — something like the Good Housekeeping seal — and a few Web retailers are setting up such guarantees.

Consumers can also take their own safeguards. Try to know your seller. When buying online, use a credit card that allows you to contest any charges and limits your liability.

Both consumers and sellers are at risk when trading on the Web. For sellers, distant shipping addresses, credit card addresses that don't match the shipping destination, and instructions like "no signature is required" are all warning signs of a possible scam. Fraudulent transactions can occur because you cannot see the seller and the seller cannot see you, check your signature, or check your photo identification. Anonymity makes fraud easy. *Net Commerce Magazine* has estimated that more than seven billion dollars was lost to theft on the Web in 1998. With the continued increase in dollar volume, the increase in theft is likely to skyrocket.

## Protecting Personal Data

Theft of proprietary information, virus contamination, and financial fraud are additional contributors to the

## Security on the Web

net crime situation. Hacker groups are of great concern. Hackers can break into Websites and have commandeered the New York Times Web site and many others. There is great vulnerability in various software programs. As these vulnerabilities are discovered, corrections are issued, but often not in time to allow computer users to avoid major problems. In the hope that it will result in a great increase in security for everyone using the World Wide Web, a new security plan is being developed by the Internet Engineering Task Force.

Eight leading Internet companies are planning a public service announcement program to teach consumers about their online privacy rights, and several plans of ways to police the industry have been developed.

A "firewall" in a building is a wall made of cinderblock or some other fireproof material intended to stop a fire from spreading. In computer lingo, firewalls act as barriers to keep away users without proper passwords in some Websites and software programs. Firewalls can be set up between parties to protect information. Other ways to keep information secure include intrusion detection, encryption, digital signatures, and hacker shields.

Encryption converts numbers and text into a secure code that is difficult to break, thus protecting the information. PGP (Pretty Good Privacy), a lightweight encryption protocol, has been produced as an industry standard. (If you're interested in learning more about privacy technology, the following Websites have up-to-date information: Electronic Privacy Information, Filtering Software, and The Privacy Journal.)

Another way to protect your private information is to make sure you don't give it away! When on the Web, make sure you don't disclose information you wish to keep private.

## Protecting Children

Parents are concerned that their children will type the word "sex" into their computer and generate tens of thousands of sites. As of this writing, the proposed federal Child Online Protection Law was under debate. The law may require Website operators to get parental permission before collecting personal information from children. It would also restrict access to harmful material. The problem is finding a way to both protect children and protect free speech rights.

# CHAPTER 7

## Making Friends on the Web

The Internet and the World Wide Web can help you make new friends and stay in touch with old friends. You can start by e-mailing friends and family members. It's a great way to stay in touch. Then you can use message boards, chat groups, and conference rooms to expand the circle of people with whom you exchange ideas and information.

A message board lets you post news and information you want to exchange with other people. Message boards are listed by topic and if you don't find one you want to join, you can start one. Chat groups are also listed by topic and are usually limited to about twenty people. Joining a chat group allows you to become friends with a roomful of strangers. New groups are being formed all the time. Conference groups are also listed by topic, but they are larger than chat groups. Other ways to exchange information and make friends include public rooms, member rooms, news groups, and virtual auditoriums where thousands of people can communicate.

## How It Works

E-mail is the most basic and important Internet service and the number one use of the Internet. A system of thousands of computer networks connected via fiber-optic cables, e-mail is mainly sent from a sending unit to a receiving unit (in most cases from computer to computer over a network connected to the Internet). The sender types in the recipient's e-mail address (say, jones@aol.com) in the appropriate box, writes a message, and hits "send." The graphics on e-mail programs are fairly self-explanatory.

E-mail can be sent anywhere in the world and can be printed on a printer. You can use a spell checker and attach files and photos to your e-mail message. This can be accomplished through the "attach file" function of the e-mail program, which may be represented graphically by a paper clip. Once a sender clicks on the "attach file" command or icon, the computer will ask for the name of the file the sender wishes to attach. The sender can then find that file — perhaps an image of a grandchild — and send it along with the e-mail. Messages sent to a wrong address can be returned.

## Making Friends on the Web 63

Generally, mail is retained in the system for two to three weeks.

Internet addresses are like postal service addresses — they tell the computer where to deliver the message. Many people use their first initial and last name as part of their e-mail address. They may not want to be gender specific since this identification is used to communicate with chat groups, message boards, and conferences.

Instant messages (IMs) work only if the sender and the receiver are online at the same time. IM-ing allows two people to communicate in real time. As you read the message on your monitor, you can be sending your answer. AOL, Microsoft MSN, Prodigy, and Yahoo offer this service. ICQ is a software program that tells you when the person to whom you want to send an instant message is online. Both parties need to use the ICQ software for this to work. The software also lets you play games and add voice. Soon everybody will be talking. Voice-enabled computers with the proper software make this possible. A few chat groups that offer this service are: www.beecall.com, www.excite.com/communities/chat/voice chat, www.paltalk.com, and www.tribalvoice.

Here are a few definitions of terms you'll probably hear as you use e-mail, chat rooms, and other Internet methods of communication:

- FTP is a software program that allows machines to exchange information;

## Chapter 7

- URL is the uniform resource locator of addresses on the Web. As an example: http//www. (Your Name)@aol would be your address if you used AOL service;
- http or hypertext transfer protocol tells your browser where to go;
- LAN means local area network.

---

Subj: **greetings**
Date: 2/3 2:11:27 PM Eastern Standard Time
From: mary@ .com
To: john@ .com

Hi Dad
I am really glad to see that you are now hooked up to the internet and using e-mail. This can be a great way to stay in touch. We took the girls to the Ice Show last night and they loved it. Send my love to mom.
Love, Mary

---

Example of e-mail page.

# CHAPTER 8

# *Advertising on the Web*

*Many of the business sites on the Web expect to generate most of their profits from advertisers paying for space on their sites, just as television has commercials. Advertising on the Web may be essential to the growth and success of the World Wide Web, which is why we have devoted this chapter to an explanation of advertising on the Web.*

No one is sure of the best way to use the Internet for advertising. In the beginning some sites put banners (signs) on their Websites, which advertised various places to go on the WWW. Their success was measured by how many people clicked on to that site. However, there did not seem to be any relationship between clicking on to a site and staying on it long enough to make a decision to purchase or to use the information. One of the most popular sites was the weather report.

In an attempt to lure retailers to the Internet, Proctor and Gamble has brought together a group of experts in various forms of advertising to discuss how to use the Internet for advertising. So far, there have been no definitive answers, but many people are working on the problem. Proctor and Gamble is concerned with the costs and wants Web costs to compare favorably with television costs. AOL has a cooperative agreement with Proctor & Gamble.

But companies aren't waiting for studies to tell them the best way to go online — they are already testing the potential of the Internet. Calvin Klein has gone online with a series of hip ads designed to promote their fragrances. Budweiser is using the Internet to promote its Super Bowl campaign. Marketers are joining the At Home Corporation: An Internet Service to create and test larger and more elaborate types of online advertising. These companies include: AT &T, Bank of America, First USA, Intel, Johnson & Johnson, Levi Strauss, and Toys 'R' Us. The marketers will run ads that use so-called "rich media" techniques such as video, sound, and animation.

Another type of ad is called a live banner. It makes it possible to purchase something that is advertised on a banner without having to leave the network. In other words, you don't have to go from where you are to

Amazon.com in order to buy a book. This exciting development allows you to instantly purchase the item you select.

Advertisers have always needed to measure the results of their advertising. Media Metrics and Relevant Knowledge, two rivals in the business of measuring audiences for advertising, have agreed to resolve their differences by merging. The move comes in response to advertisers who wanted a single measuring tool for the Internet as they currently have on TV with the Nielsen Company.

TV and media ads for companies that market their products through the Internet are increasing as these companies realize that they need to use traditional media in order to gain viewers for their ads on the Internet. You can see the "www" Web addresses on the sides of buses, on television commercials, and on billboards. Likewise, it's easy for a company to place its e-mail address and URL (Website address) information on its letterhead and business cards. This tactic again serves to remind people about a company's WWW presence and Internet capabilities.

If a company currently advertises its products in any high-tech magazines, it will definitely benefit from listing its electronic access information. Audiences of those magazines generally access the Internet and appreciate knowing a company's web address.

A company should also include its e-mail and WWW addresses on any catalogs that it might produce. If a company allows people to fax their orders, its e-mail address and URL should be listed alongside the fax number. If users have a fax machine, they quite possibly have Internet access as well.

Because of the initial popularity of the Internet, companies that promote their Internet presence early will benefit the most from the novelty. After a few years when most businesses are hooked up to e-mail and WWW pages are prevalent, it will be considered unusual for a company not to list its Web address.

## Internet: The Next Advertising Medium

Typically, new media have done a few key things better than older media. For example, newspapers were better than town criers because the information was recorded. Magazines were better than newspapers because they focused more on national issues (and had high quality pictures). Radio was better than magazines because it was live. Television was better than radio because it added moving pictures. Internet is better than television because it provides live sound, both still and moving pictures, and timely information and entertainment when users want it, with the powerful addition of interactivity.

Usually, new media evolutions have initially been held back by the deployment of appropriate receivers.

## Advertising on the Web 69

The evolution of newspapers was limited by low literacy levels and high production costs. Magazine usage growth was constrained by the same issues, plus high distribution costs. Radio and television usage growth was initially restricted by the high costs of radio and television receivers. Cable television usage growth was restricted by the deployment of high-cost coaxial cable. Internet growth is governed by the cost of PCs and the cost of high-speed Internet access. But low-speed access is reasonably priced (sometimes free) and the cost of computers is dropping rapidly. Web TV offers access to the Web at a lower hardware cost because it uses your TV set as the receiver to make getting on the Web easy.

For advertisers, each new medium has offered new opportunities. Newspapers offered local markets and an audience focused on making purchases. Magazines offered both a narrower market focus (and thus a more segmented, targeted audience) and larger (even national) audiences. Radio delivered real-time information (locally and nationally), replete with the ability to generate more effective advertising through the use of sound. TV just added pictures to the sound.

The Internet adds the element of interactivity and the ability to make purchases within the medium. It's the only medium in which a user can see an advertisement, inquire about the product/service quickly or in detail, make an immediate purchase, and save time and money.

## Advantages of Web Advertising over Traditional Advertising

The following is a list of the major advantages offered by Web advertising over traditional advertising:

- Instant high global visibility;
- A rich medium for multimedia content;
- A chance for small companies to compete against much bigger players on an even playing field;
- Easy-to-use feedback forms;
- Interactive Websites, which demonstrate the product or service or provide a virtual reality walk-through, in which the user could interact with the advertisement;
- Flexibility, in that a company's Web advertisement could change every day, even though a company usually pays for an advertisement to be carried for an entire year. In fact, Websites that do not change often do not get many visitor responses;
- Online billing and, in the case of products like software, online delivery. A credit card billing facility could be built into the Website, if the server and the bank both support it. Many banks do, and some even offer a direct debit service for one to use from a company's own Web page;
- Online reservations. Central reservation systems that are globally accessible could be built with little expense.

## Users of Web Advertisements

The following groups could have much to gain from Internet advertisements:

- Anyone seeking international business for a product or a service;
- Anyone looking for Internet-related work;
- The service industry. Work samples can be displayed online, and orders may even be executed over the Internet;
- Hotels, the tourism industry, and travel agencies;
- Services that can justify online reservations and exhibition space booking;
- Insurance, real estate, and banking;
- Activist organizations, since the Web is an inexpensive way to reach a large audience;
- Groups scheduling conferences and seminars, so that parallel virtual conferences could be held on the Web and more people can attend and participate without having to be physically present;
- Advertisers of sports events and award ceremonies, so they can reach a wider audience with assured high visibility at a low cost;
- Educators, who could teach for free, with a large outreach;
- Governmental and regulatory bodies, which would benefit from providing easily accessible information about rules and regulations, facilities for international business, and other information;

- Job and project marketers who would have an easy way to offer jobs and projects with all specifications, including international requests;
- Companies wanting to promote an international image — being on the Web makes looking for a joint venture and partners easier for overseas investors.

## The World of Multimedia Advertising

Many companies want to combine their existing advertising with their Internet presence. National or international companies will probably want to mirror their print and television advertising in their Web pages. Slogans, jingles, colors, and styles can be changed to reflect new advertising campaigns. Promotions and contests can be mirrored on the Internet to provide alternative methods for users to enter drawings.

The Internet opened new doors to many companies. Many businesses never dreamed that they could have full-color advertising with worldwide distribution. This new media capability allows companies to show products and offer services in ways they never could before.

## How to Advertise on the Web

When a company places an advertisement in a magazine, newspaper, or on TV, people reading that publication or watching that station will see it's an advertisement. On the Web, however, a company must make the customer come to its advertisement. The consumer must type the URL or choose the link.

In traditional advertising, the success of an advertisement depends on not only how the advertisement looks, but also in what magazine it appears or during what TV program it is shown. Likewise, the success of a company's WWW advertising will depend on where and how it promotes its product as well as how it looks. In order to promote its advertisement, a company must give something extra to the people who visit its site, such as discounts, gifts, or information.

## How the Advertisements Are Made

How and where graphics are used depends on what type of impact a company wants to make. This section will describe some, but not all, of the types of advertising used on the Internet. We won't go into too much detail in this general-interest book — if you are interested in more information on how to advertise on the Internet, bookstores are loaded with books about this subject.

### *Moving graphics*

Moving graphics offer businesses the ability to display detailed visual information about their products. For example, a car manufacturer can show video clips over the Internet, demonstrating how a car operates on winding roads. The movie is downloaded into the user's machine and played at full speed from the system.

Currently, the use of moving pictures in Internet advertising is rare. This is because with existing connections, downloading a video takes too much time. For example, a video of five minutes with the most common 33.6 megahertz connection takes about ten minutes to download. In the future, cable connection will reduce the time to about one minute.

### *Hyperlink and Other References*

The WWW is really all about linking. If users could not link, they would not be able to move from place to place. Linking provides a company with the ability to have its information organized in pieces that can more accurately present its data. Most pages have a statement of links and often provide the linked e-mail address of the page's creator.

### *Virtual Reality*

Currently, the hardware (such as a helmet and input gloves) used to implement virtual reality is clumsy and the images are not real-world quality, but two-dimensional video brochures on the Internet turn into three-dimensional versions of the places they represent. Bars will look like bars, hotels will look like hotels, etc., with unlimited design options.

## Web Advertising Methods

In his book *Confessions of an Advertising Man*, David Ogilvy wrote, "The market you are advertising to is not just a crowd, but a passing parade." While these words aptly summarize the nature of all media, they seem especially appropriate for the Internet.

At its core, Internet advertising is similar to many other forms of advertising — it's all about reaching potential customers and making an impression. And as in any business, advertisers on the Internet want to maximize profit by selling as much product as possible and in any way possible. Well-designed advertising that is creative and delivered in the right environment is a key driver of advertising success. It is important that ads not be too intrusive because the more an advertisement seems like a value-added service to the user and less like an invasion of privacy, the more successful that advertisement will be in driving traffic or business to wherever it is connected. An example would be a drug company that offers health information as part of its advertising. At the opposite extreme is "spam," which refers to the practice by some advertisers of sending unsolicited, mass-mailed e-mail advertisements. Although some Internet users don't seem to mind receiving this type of advertisement, the majority has been vocal in their complaints.

This brings us back to the concept of links, which basically are anything on a Web page that drives traffic to another site. Links can be presented in the form of buttons, hypertext, advertising banners, or something else, but they all provide pathways from one Website to another, and are major drivers of site traffic.

An example of a Web page and analysis of the various Web-advertising products and methods follows:

### Banners

Banners are by far the most common advertising products sold on the Web, and most companies have adopted this product for the majority of the advertising they sell. Banner advertisements can be thought of as mini-billboards for advertisers on the information superhighway.

Typically, a banner advertisement is a horizontal, rectangular graphic image appearing at the top of a Web page, and often using GIP, Java, or Shockwave animations. The banner usually includes some text, such as a phrase or slogan and the advertiser's name and Internet address. If the user finds the advertisement intriguing enough, he or she will then click on the advertisement, which activates an embedded link, to visit the advertiser's Website.

One could think of the Web page being downloaded as a postcard and the banner advertisement as a stamp. As the page is delivered, it is just like slapping the stamp on the postcard as it goes out to the post office (the Internet) to be delivered to the addressee (the user). The method of selecting the advertisement (stamp) to be added to each page is handled by advertisement management software.

## Buttons

Another Web advertising product offered by Web publishers is a "button" on their pages. Buttons are advertisements for software products such as Netscape Navigator and Microsoft's Internet Explorer (browser clients), Macromedia's Shockwave software, and PointCast's client software. Each of these companies pays an Internet service provider a royalty for placing its button on a page that, if the user clicks on it, will take the user to the company's download site. We believe this is direct marketing at its finest.

Clicking on that button takes the user to a "Featured Product" page, where he or she can read a description of the product and access links to download the software directly.

## Key Words

Search engines, by definition, use text input by users to conduct searches of relevant content on the Web. Since advertisements are displayed along with the search results, these companies allow advertisers to buy "key words" which display the advertiser's banner when a user searches for that word ("sailboats," for example). It follows that the word or words purchased are generally related in some way to the advertiser's products or services.

## Direct E-mail

Direct e-mail is a technique used to keep a Website's products fresh in users' minds. This is an opportunity for companies to reverse the normal "pull" methodology of Internet surfing (in which the users have to go out and find the content) to more of a "push" paradigm (in which advertisers take the content to the users).

Many sites use interesting ploys to obtain a user's e-mail address, and then leverage this knowledge by sending e-mails that detail updates of the site, promotions, newsletters, and so on. Sites also can sell their user information (along with any other demographic details) to marketing firms, which use them for other direct marketing campaigns.

## Creating Traffic on a Company's Website

Traffic can be created from numerous Internet sources through dozens of tried-and-true, traffic-generating tips and techniques. The most common is the strategic use of search engines and directories.

The users start their search for what they need with one of these powerful tools. A query to find a company or subject may generate twenty thousand hits, and few users bother searching past the first one hundred. They choose from the top fifty or so selections, and usually the top ten. So a company must concentrate on getting a high placement. On the Internet, there are hundreds of search engines and directories. Many of them are very poorly trafficked, or have an extremely specialized audience. Almost everyone agrees that the top ten search engines and directories are responsible for the vast majority of traffic on the Internet. So, the single most important thing a company can do to create traffic is to get high placement on the top search engines. This isn't quite as simple as adding "A"s to the beginning of your company name (as in "A #1 Pizzeria" ) in order to get top placement in the Yellow Pages. It is possible to control placement on Internet search engines and directories, though the discussion of how to do it is best left to more technical books.

## Winners

A "sticky" Website is one on which the surfer spends a lot of time. The more time a surfer spends on a site, the more opportunities the site operator has to show advertising and make a sale.

Among the stickiest are:

- eBay.com, the online auction;
- Yahoo.com: Internet directory, shopping, and e-mail;
- Schwab.com: stock trading and research.

Among companies that provide Web access, four have emerged as superpowers in terms of number of surfers. They are America Online, Yahoo/Geocities, Microsoft, and USA/LYCOS. More than half of all Internet users visit the Yahoo site.

## Chapter 8

These companies are engaged in a battle to be first with the most viewers and the longest stickiness.

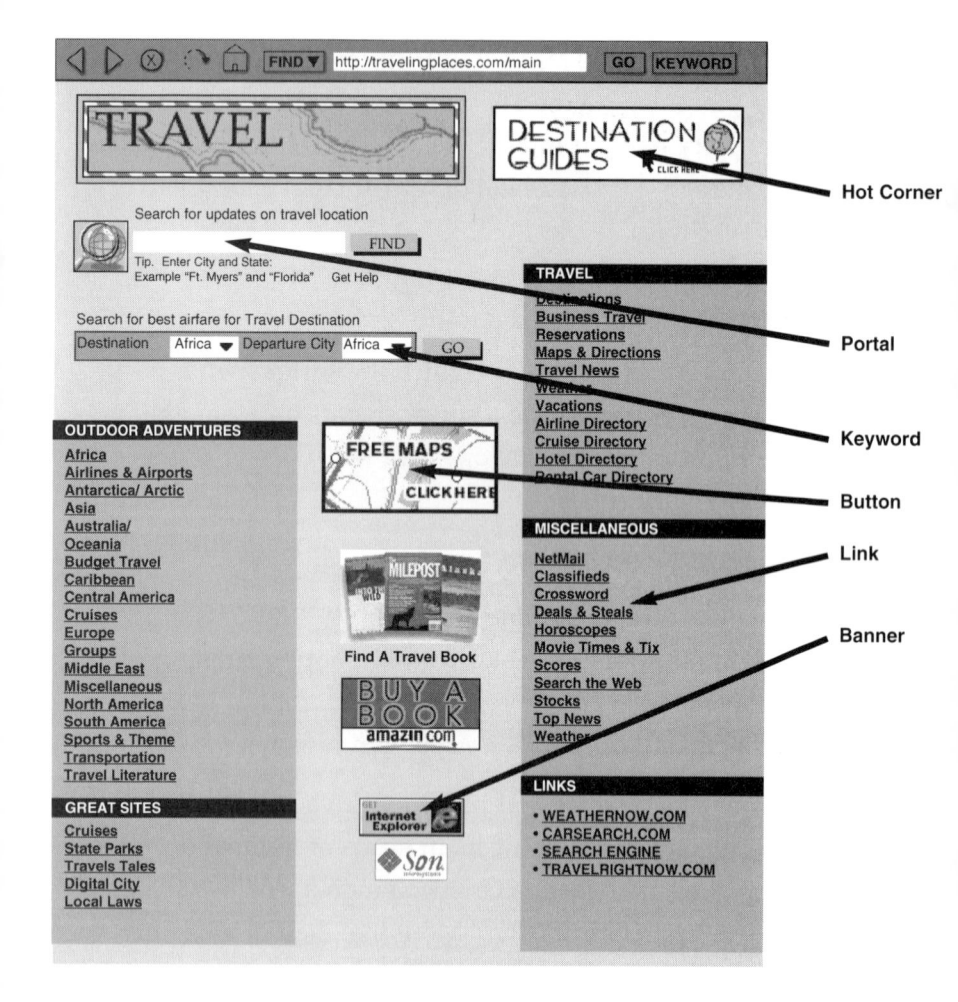

# CHAPTER 9

## And More

### Education

Distance learning — learning at home, while traveling, or while on vacation — is the new way to get an advanced degree, all made possible through the Internet. An advanced degree earned through a distance learning program will look just like any other degree. The number of schools offering distance learning programs and the number of courses you can take is almost unlimited. For example, at this writing Duke University offers an MBA; The University of North London offers an MA; Oxford University in England offers two non-degree courses; Stanford University offers a masters in electrical engineering; Harvard

University offers a computer course; Seton Hall University offers two graduate programs, one in health care and one in executive communications; and DePaul University of Chicago offers a course on the Internet. The University of Illinois offers a graduate program in library science. Some instructors are offering courses on their own and it is now possible to get a law degree from Kaplan Law School via the Web. MBA students have been taking Internet Marketing classes because this skill promises jobs and big salaries.

Microsoft Corporation and the Massachusetts Institute of Technology have formed a partnership called I-Campus. Projects include distance learning and Internet publishing.

Online courses reach students beyond the university's walls. In fact, they reach all over the world. It is possible for a student attending the University of Illinois's graduate program in library science to have classmates in Oregon and Argentina. Many colleges see this as a new stream of profits, which will make possible improvements in their schools and their courses. This whole new area of education is expanding rapidly. We can expect that students will have to decide whether they want the experience of an away or at home education. We think that for many the deciding factor will be the cost, because the cost of staying at home is often so much cheaper.

## Charity — The Pleasure Of Giving

The Web provides a tremendous amount of information on how to give to charity. Many people give a percentage of their income each year — some as much as ten percent. In order to do this well, it is important to develop a plan of giving because there are so many needy charities. A concentration of effort will improve results.

A Website called the Guide Store provides information on six hundred thousand charities. Other Websites that provide information about charities include The Better Business Bureau, The Council On Foundations, and The United Way. (A charity Website can be a way to reach out to the needy, not just potential donors — the United Way donated the space on its Web page and gave approval to First Call for a help database line that would provide help to people in need.)

Perhaps one of the best ways to manage money for charity is through one of the stock funds (such as Fidelity and Merrill Lynch) that hold and distribute money to charities for donors. It is surprising how many charities there are, even in a local market. For example, Florida's Sarasota and Manatee counties have more than 340 nonprofit organizations and 1,200 programs.

The Rockefeller Foundation offers a course in philanthropy to train young philanthropists who have inherited wealth or earned a great deal of money.

New Tithing, a San Francisco group, is devoted to increasing charitable giving among wealthy Americans.

Bill Gates, Chairman of Microsoft, has donated more than eleven billion dollars to establish foundations interested in global education and health.

## Information — News on the Web

The WWW is an important source of news. In 1998, Americans saw the power of the WWW as a news source with the rapid transmission of the Starr Report — former independent counsel Ken Starr's report on the affair between President Bill Clinton and an intern, Monica Lewinsky.

In the first twenty-four hours that the U.S. Congress published the report on its Website, 750,000 people downloaded it. Fourteen million people had access to it through America Online. The pressure of a twenty-four-hour news cycle put this report in the hands of Americans everywhere without any regard for how explicit sexual material in the report should be handled. Chat rooms were filled with people wanting to talk about it and bulletin boards were full of notes. Apparently, the Net has become the soapbox of our time. Seven million additional people visited the Starr Report via CNN, MSNBC, The House of Representatives, Library of Commerce, Yahoo, ABC News, Government Printing Office, Microsoft, USA Today, X-Site, Fax News, Fox News, and other sources, with absolutely overwhelming results.

The president put his rebuttal on the Internet and it also was read by millions of people. The Web proved itself to be an instant conveyor of news to all Americans and maintained its place at the threshold of new information systems.

## Sex on the Web

The video cassette recorder spawned a whole new sex industry by allowing middle-class Americans who would never go to a blue movie house to watch X-rated videos in the privacy of their homes. The Web allows people access to sexual materials with an even greater degree of discretion — you don't even have to let the clerk at the video store know what you're doing.

There are thousands of sex sites in the United States and millions of Americans visit a sex site regularly. There are more hits on sex than on sports or the news. And visitors are not just visiting the sites in the privacy of their own homes. It has been reported that two-thirds of the companies that monitor their employees on the Web found they were surfing sex sites while on the job. Many of the sites become overloaded at the end of the college day.

Hundreds of sex bulletin boards, thousands of sex e-mail messages, and nude photos are available free online. The largest site is Sex.com, which has revenues of a hundred million dollars a year. Thousands of home-based sites lose money while hoping for a big break.

86 | Chapter 9

Government and industry attempts to protect children from these sites have not been completely successful because of our free speech rights. This is discussed more fully in Chapter 3.

Example of an online advertisement for computer training courses.

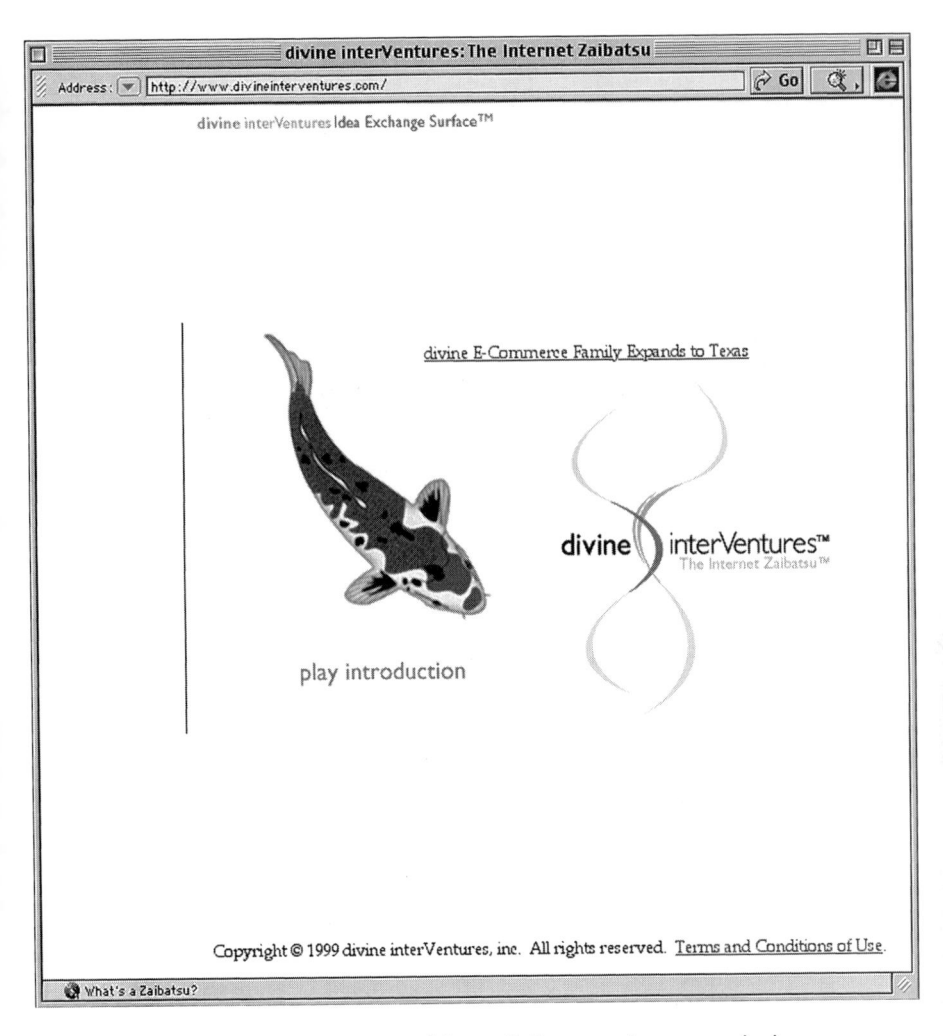

# And More

divine interVentures: The Internet Zaibatsu

Address: http://www.divineinterventures.com/

divine interVentures Idea Exchange Surface™

divine E-Commerce Family Expands to Texas

divine interVentures™
The Internet Zaibatsu™

play introduction

Copyright © 1999 divine interVentures, inc. All rights reserved. Terms and Conditions of Use.

What's a Zaibatsu?

Divine interVentures provides all the services needed to start a business-to-business company — know-how and money.

## Chapter 9

---

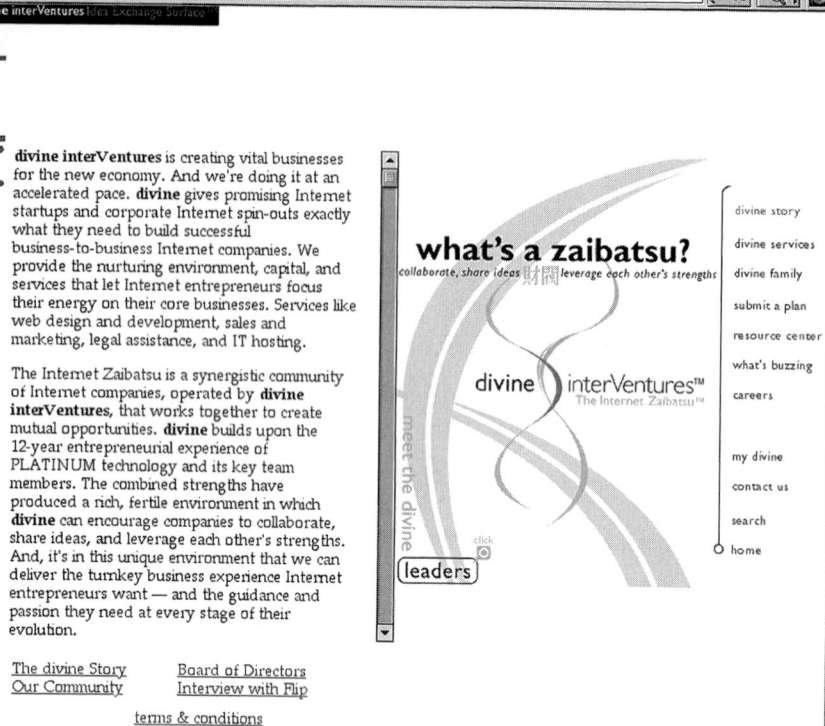

**divine interVentures: The Internet Zaibatsu**

Address: http://www.divineinterventures.com/default.asp?m=story

divine interVentures Idea Exchange Surface

### the divine story

**divine interVentures** is creating vital businesses for the new economy. And we're doing it at an accelerated pace. **divine** gives promising Internet startups and corporate Internet spin-outs exactly what they need to build successful business-to-business Internet companies. We provide the nurturing environment, capital, and services that let Internet entrepreneurs focus their energy on their core businesses. Services like web design and development, sales and marketing, legal assistance, and IT hosting.

The Internet Zaibatsu is a synergistic community of Internet companies, operated by **divine interVentures**, that works together to create mutual opportunities. **divine** builds upon the 12-year entrepreneurial experience of PLATINUM technology and its key team members. The combined strengths have produced a rich, fertile environment in which **divine** can encourage companies to collaborate, share ideas, and leverage each other's strengths. And, it's in this unique environment that we can deliver the turnkey business experience Internet entrepreneurs want — and the guidance and passion they need at every stage of their evolution.

The divine Story
Our Community

Board of Directors
Interview with Flip

terms & conditions

**what's a zaibatsu?**
collaborate, share ideas 財閥 leverage each other's strengths

divine interVentures™
The Internet Zaibatsu™

meet the divine

(leaders) click

divine story
divine services
divine family
submit a plan
resource center
what's buzzing
careers
my divine
contact us
search
home

divine Leaders

# CHAPTER 10

# The Government and the Web

## Taxes

The government has the right to tax and regulate the actions of people and businesses. Those rights often determine the success or failure of various enterprises. Perhaps nothing affects commerce more than taxes, and so far the Web has been given a free ride. The Internet Tax Freedom Act passed by the Senate guarantees no taxes on Internet transactions until 2001. This gives the Internet a considerable advantage over other sales methods and particularly over direct mail, which is presently subject to a variety of use and sales taxes. A recent study of the purchasing habits of online consumers showed that the number of online shoppers and the dollar amounts they spend would drop by almost a third if a sales tax was charged on purchases. Some states, however, had imposed taxes on Internet access and data transfers before the passage of the Act, and those taxes will remain in place. One of the suggestions for a fairer taxing method would be to go to a cash flow tax which would be charged toward all transactions whether sales originate from retail stores, direct mail, or the Internet. There will be much discussion of this in the coming years.

The legal issue regarding taxing Internet purchases is how to tax purchases that cross state lines. A sales tax *per se* can only be collected when the sale and the delivery to the buyer occur in the same state. However, an Internet company that has a presence in the same state as the buyer does have to collect sales tax even though the order is placed on the Internet and the merchandise is shipped from out of state. States cannot require sellers to collect use taxes from their out-of-state customers, and laws ban the states from interfering with interstate commerce. Nonetheless, state governments derive at least one-third of their revenue and often more from sales taxes. The National Governors Association and other government groups are worried that they will lose billions of dollars a year in normal taxable income because of sales made on the Internet. This will have a disproportionate impact on states that depend heavily on sales tax, and will benefit the affluent who have greater access to the Internet and to computers.

## Domain Name

What's a domain name? It's a name that is registered by Network Solutions Inc. the official registrar under contract with the U.S. Government. Once registered and used as a Website, the name can be maintained by paying registration fees at various intervals.

Many other countries have complained that this U.S. monopoly puts them at a disadvantage. Also, a number of other companies, such as the Domain Name Rights Coalition, want the right to offer this service.

The government has agreed to eventually hand over administration of the domain name registration system to a nonprofit corporation. Until now, Network Solutions has had an exclusive contract from the government since 1995 and will see its monopoly end by 2001. Network Solutions currently registers names with the endings of com, net, org, gov, mil, and edu. The Commerce Department has recommended adding five new top-level domains to the Web. While they have not been selected yet, likely candidates are: web, stock, store, arts, and shop.

What is a name worth? Think about Mickey Mouse, Hershey, Campbell Soup, and G.E. A good name can be worth millions because of the number of hits it can attract to its Website. Some companies have filed for hundreds of names in the hope of selling the names at a profit. Political candidates have run into this problem — they hope to open a Website to provide information about their campaign, only to find that JaneJones2000 has already been taken and is now being offered for sale. The Federal Trademark Dilution Act of 1995 makes it possible to take legal action against someone who has filed for your name on the Web in order to sell your name to you at a high price.

## Other Government Web Work

Besides controlling domain name and tax policy, the government is involved in Internet development in numerous other ways. For example, the Commerce Department and Federal Trade Commission are considering how to police the Internet, educate consumers to protect themselves from fraud, increase private investments, and encourage high-speed networks. The Commerce Department and Small Business Administration are trying to encourage small businesses to use the Web.

The White House has suggested a plan to expand Internet projects in developing nations. Included in this plan are financial assistance, small business administration loans, the development of international trade groups to establish consumer protection standards, a promise to keep the Federal Communications Commission out of cyberspace, and helping developing nations link remote areas to the Internet via satellites.

The U.S. Government and the European Economic Union countries have moved in opposite directions in protecting the privacy of the consumer. Under current planning, Europeans will be guaranteed the right to see any information collected about them, to refuse to share information for direct marketing purposes, to correct inaccuracies in their records, to gain some kind of recourse if personal information is used without permission, and to find out how that information was gathered. None of these rights are available under United States law, which has simply covered government release of information and not private industry. The result is that there may be a blockade of information to and from the United States until the question of how to regulate this area is resolved.

The protection of trademarks and patents has always been an important function of the United States government. But recently there have been important changes in how patents may be granted. We used to have basically two types of patents available: design patents and mechanical utility patents. It was impossible to patent an idea. You had to patent its artistic look or its mechanical application. The courts were hostile to the idea of patents based on ways of doing business. But a July 1998 ruling of the Federal Circuit Court of Appeals found that computerized business methods could be patented. So claiming the computer as part of a patent may make things patentable that weren't patentable before. For example, PriceLine.com Inc. of Stanford, Connecticut, was awarded a patent on reverse auctions.

If the Patent Office continues in this mode, it is likely that venture capitalists won't talk to a startup that doesn't have a patent on its ideas, which in turn is likely to generate lawsuits. Another patent claimed is the right to survey on the Web. A patent was issued on Too Cool Savings, one of seven companies distributing coupon-style discounts to consumers via the Web. The patented process involves discount certificates aimed at the most important customers.

Trademarks are under government control, and the government has recently made it easy to access its trademark database through the Patented Trademark Office's World Wide Web.

The future of the Internet will be changed in large part by two new programs. One is a government-led program called "Next Generation Internet Research," for which the government has budgeted more than one hundred million dollars per year. The second program is an industry program entitled "Internet Two," for which industry will develop faster and broader methods of Internet access.

Selective Service has added a Website so eighteen-year-old males can register. As of this writing, the United States was also investigating airline handling and pay of Web ticket agents.

In 1999, a federal judge ruled that a library couldn't filter the Internet. Freedom of speech requires that libraries allow all material on the Internet to be accessed from the library.

China is testing its grip on the Internet. It wants to screen and control what citizens access in another attempt to restrict speech.

A number of proposals for allowing Americans to be able to vote using the Internet instead of having to go to a polling booth have been debated.

Perhaps the most exciting government action involving the Internet in recent years has been the landmark Microsoft monopoly trial and subsequent settlement negotiations, because they involve most computer and Internet companies. The trial and settlement negotiations will help determine who gains control of the computer and Internet market.

**96** Chapter 10

Example of a local Website for regional information.

# CHAPTER 11

## *Web Technology and the Future*

The Web is not a flash in the pan — it is a development like the printing press that is creating a revolution in our lifetimes. Change on the Internet is so fast that no one can predict the outcome, except to say that it will continue to change every aspect of how we live and work. It will continue to grow in importance as an advertising medium, a communication network, an information center, a shopping mall, and a meeting place. Future innovations to the Web will make it work faster and more efficiently, and will address current problems like slow transmissions and security concerns. The following are descriptions of developing Internet technologies, and some crystal-ball predictions of what the future will bring.

## Chapter 11

Search engines are growing in the Internet business. People who use the Web say it takes too much time to locate the information they want. Search engines provide a solution. They find the sites that have the information you want by matching key words you enter into the search area. Almost no one wants to click through hundreds of matches to find the one they want. Companies that offer a search service include: Alta Vista (one of the ten most visited Websites); Northern Light Technology, which has an index of more than 160 million Web pages; Yahoo; and Lycos, Inc. www.hotbot.com finds popular sites, and MSN.com and AOL.com have improved search engines.

Altavista has made searching the Web easier by allowing you to search for specific types of responses. This includes searching the Web with a keyword or keywords for images, audio clips, screen savers, Websites, or all of the above. They have also made basic searching more user friendly by allowing surfers to search a question for i.e. "Where can I find Lincoln's birthplace?"

www.Guronet.com lets you click on words and brings up all information related to those words. www.couple.com determines the importance of a page to the subject you are searching and puts you into that site. i-won.com is an Internet search directory that offers registered users a chance to win in their daily, monthly, and grand prize drawings every time they click on the site.

In the future, it is expected that search engines will become more focused, so that users will not pull up

## Web Technology and the Future | 99

hundreds of useless matches. Internet filtering software can tell parents what their children watch. It can tell employers what their employees are watching and it can obstruct access to selected sites.

Internet technology that lets computers talk to each other also makes it possible to allow interaction between any items that can hold a computer chip, including copiers, cameras, air conditioners, cars, and other useful connectors.

The deployment of broad band networks offers the Internet multimedia uses. ION (Integrated On-Demand Network) gathers data, voice, and video networks in one easy-to-manage system. Internet telephone products let users place overseas calls for a fraction of phone costs.

3 COM Corp. has introduced a new version that allows wireless access to the Internet. A number of phone manufacturers have introduced phones that connect to the Internet. Some are combination phone and palm devices.

A new high-speed telephone cable system will offer service across the Atlantic at speeds twenty-five times the current capacity.

ICQ is a technology that allows messages and voice in real time and an increased speed over phone lines. It has thousands of chat rooms on the widest range of subjects.

Modems connect users to the Internet, and the new multi-modem ISI allows more users to connect at greater speeds.

Talk Net Radio.com plans to offer the technology to start your own talk show on the Net. Service is free, but limited to groups of thirty.

Media Highway System provides millions of European households with ultra-fast interactive digital TV. You can customize your services, download software, and surf the Internet. The systems can hook up to TV sets, VCRs, camcorders, scanners, and portable phones — all without the use of a personal computer.

We believe that telephone service soon will be provided by Internet access providers and cable TV companies. Wireless Application Protocol (WAP) phones transmit voice and data.

Ordinary phone lines have a maximum speed of 26,400 bits per second. COMPAQ Computer has introduced a modem that works with a DSL (Digital) phone line with a speed of 384,000 bits per second. Comcast and other cable companies offer high speed Internet access at one hundred times the usual modem connection. ADSL (Asymmetrical Digital Subscriber Lines) is two hundred times faster than today's phone modems. This service is expanding across the USA. ISDN (Integrated Services Digital Network) processes at speeds of eight million bits per second or four hundred times as fast as the usual phone line.

Satellites will provide broadband, "streaming" Internet and television services. Streaming is a cost-effective personalized method of distributing information.

## Web Technology and the Future

Speech recognition will come to the aid of those who don't want to type and will make it possible to identify the caller for added security.

AOL TV, a service of America Online, will compete with WEB TV and expects to have millions of subscribers.

In the future, fingerprint readers will make passwords unnecessary. You will just put your finger on a reader on the keypad and send the picture — no typing, no long numbers, etc. Consumers' fear of fraud will decrease as fingerprint identification takes hold.

The Internet will merge with phones and TV sets. Hand-held devices will combine audio, pictures, and data.

Higher bandwidths will make communication faster.

Computers will continue to be an important connection because prices will decrease and capacity will increase, but TV-connected devices will grow in importance.

Consumers and suppliers will become information partners, improving traditional communication.

The Web will be dominated by a dozen top companies followed by thousands of special niches.

Many successful companies will obtain up to half of their sales online.

Everyone will be able to use the Internet as equipment and usage will become almost free.

The Internet will become the most cost-driven system ever devised. Retailing will progress to a very low markup on costs. Distribution of goods and services will rely on advertising income to provide total income.

Electronic billing systems will save merchants and banks billions of dollars, and consumers will experience a new level of convenience. This will have a serious impact on the business of the U.S. Post Office, since more than half of first class mail consists of bills and payments.

Electronic books are increasingly being used by schools and colleges because of improved visibility on the monitor and improved speed of access. The cost of a book online could be one dollar versus ten dollars for a printed version.

Home delivery services will experience rapid growth as sales increase on the Internet. This will require better facilities for the safe receipt of large packages — a mailbox just won't be good enough anymore. Apartment buildings, for example, will need to have areas just for the receipt of packages. Every home will need a "safe box" for the receipt of packages.

With hundreds of thousands of Websites, there are growing demands for various levels of service. Just as Federal Express offers various levels of service (next day service, second day service, etc.), the Internet could provide various levels of service to fit different needs and different budgets.

# Web Technology and the Future

Satellite communication will provide global access to the Internet, fax capabilities, paging, and voice communication at faster speeds and lower costs.

There will be no more simple "home" pages — everyone will be constructing not just a home, but a lushly decorated palace using interactive tools.

The government, computer industry, and one hundred universities have already started the Internet 2/A project to develop a more advanced Internet.

The future predictions of Jupiter Communications and Forrester Research are that eighty-five million Americans will shop online and spend seventy-eight billion dollars, and that advertisers will spend twenty-four billion dollars to advertise on the Web.

We hope this book will help you prepare for the new world of the Web.

Here's to health, wealth, and friends — Cheers.

The Authors

## Author Biographies

**Niall G. Caldwell** was born in Belfast, Northern Ireland. He is currently a senior lecturer in Marketing at the University of North London. He received his Ph.D. from Stony Brook University, New York, and his M.B.A. in finance and Marketing from the University of Chicago. Before joining the faculty at North London, he worked as an account manager for a Saatchi & Saatchi Agency in Chicago.

**Georgios I. Petalotis** was born in Serres, Greece. He received his degree in business administration from the Technological Institute of Serres. He was awarded a masters degree in marketing from the University of North London. His current research interests include Internet advertising, marketing communications, and small-to-medium business management.

**Ronald H. Taub** was born in New York. He received his undergraduate degree from New York University, a masters of science degree from the National College of Education, and an hPh.D. from Spertus College. He was chairman of one of the marketing agencies of Saatchi and Saatchi Advertising — Marketing Services Group, Creative Displays. He is president of Taub Enterprises, Inc., a marketing, manufacturing, and sales company.